CW00554838

TRENT LOCK, SHARDLOW AND THE EREWASH CANAL

TRENT LOCK, SHARDLOW AND THE EREWASH CANAL

KEITH TAYLOR

TEMPUS

First published 2007

Tempus Publishing Limited
The Mill, Brimscombe Port,
Stroud, Gloucestershire, GL5 2QG
www.tempus-publishing.com

© Keith Taylor, 2007

The right of Keith Taylor to be identified as the Author
of this work has been asserted in accordance with the
Copyrights, Designs and Patents Act 1988.

All rights reserved. No part of this book may be reprinted
or reproduced or utilised in any form or by any electronic,
mechanical or other means, now known or hereafter invented,
including photocopying and recording, or in any information
storage or retrieval system, without the permission in writing
from the Publishers.

British Library Cataloguing in Publication Data.
A catalogue record for this book is available from the British Library.

ISBN 978 0 7524 4321 8

Typesetting and origination by Tempus Publishing Limited.
Printed in Great Britain.

CONTENTS

	Introduction	7
	Acknowledgements	9
1	The Resourceful Rivers	11
2	The People of the Past	19
3	The Canal Boats and Horses	25
4	Around Trent Lock	31
5	Within Living Memory	37
6	Along the Erewash Canal	55
7	Langley Mill – Great Northern Basin	83
8	Downstream of Trent Lock	91
9	Upstream of Trent Lock	99
10	Trent Lock in the Twenty-First Century	103
11	Trent & Mersey Canal	113
12	Shardlow's Pubs and Village	119
	Bibliography	127

INTRODUCTION

This compilation of stories and reminiscences on the Trent Lock and Erewash Canal is a product of my interest in the waterways of Great Britain, their histories and the unique forms of employment and transportation associated with them. However, I must admit that I am not an expert on any single waterway; in truth, I would best be described as a towpath enthusiast and waterways explorer.

Since boyhood I have enjoyed walking by the waterways, especially those close to home. I also gain satisfaction from delving into the archives in the hope of discovering interesting aspects of the craftsmanship, employment, social history and leisure facilities that give each separate route its distinctive sense of purpose and regional character. This remains as much the case today as it ever was in the past.

Having spent my 1940s' boyhood within walking distance of the by-then derelict Nottingham Canal, I have always been aware of the canal's importance to our industrial past. In particular I was close to the arm striking off from Lenton Chain to bypass the Wollaton Colliery and was always aware of the staircase of lock gates that had been abandoned there. In a way they served as exhibits in my own personal, but much-neglected, museum of transportation and social history.

How many generations of gnarled and chapped hands had worked this or that windlass, I used to wonder? How big were the boats? How well kept were the horses? And how did the boat people dress and sound?

In the summer of 1954 I cycled several towpaths to locations like Gunthorpe Lock on the River Trent and followed the Derby Canal to Shelton Lock. A stifling Friday evening was forecast for Trent Lock, Long Eaton, that year in August. From the Nottingham suburb of Aspley a friend and I connected with the A453, cycled through Long Eaton, then turned along the towpath of the Erewash Canal at the Tamworth Road bridge. On that, our first, visit we saw no one. From the railway bridges, almost through to the Mill Dockyard bridge, reeds and brambles flanked the waterway. Moorhens swimming across to them appeared to be the canal's only residents, although there were several moored boats, as indeed there are today. There were no cooling towers and a deserted River Trent reflected the fires of the sunset. The sense of the place having been abandoned was almost tangible.

From that time Trent Lock seemed a good place to be heading when I was cycling with my girlfriend, but it was not until I took a job in Long Eaton during the mid-1960s that the reminiscences of the local folk gradually gave me an idea of the sense of identity felt by the people who populated the 11¾ miles from Trent Lock to the Great Northern Basin, then on to Shardlow. Since then I have spoken with boatmen, maintenance crews, lengthmen, lock-keepers, railwaymen and local folk, most of who have had a tale to tell about Trent Lock and the surrounding waterways. The late Ike Argeant gave me several copies of photographs from his collection, along with an account of his busy and colourful life which answered many of my questions, including that on the kind of people who had turned the rusted windlass.

My several visits to the Stoke Bruerne Canal Museum in Northamptonshire gave me a further insight into the workings of our waterways, I found out about the criss-cross patterning of routes and the skills involved in erecting lock gates. A visit to Gloucester Docks was equally educational. Here I learned about the tack used for horses, knitting fenders and much else besides.

A couple of years ago I called for coffee at The Lock House Tea Rooms, Trent Lock, and my interest in waterway histories grew. Here I learned how much effort the Ashbys had put in to interpreting those intriguing aspects of waterways history that had been represented between the four walls of their award-winning tea rooms.

River Erewash at the Shipley Viaduct.

recorded. What is known is that narrowboats were using the water-filled canal from the Trent to Ilkeston Common by the following April.

By July the narrowboats were completing the journey between the Trent and Langley Bridge in both directions. Boats with beams of 14ft 6ins were successfully negotiating the fourteen sets of wide gauge lock gates. However, this practice would not be run on a fully commercial basis for a further four or five months, although the reason for this delay has been lost. It is not certain whether manpower or horsepower was used at first to take the narrowboats along the canal; official authorisation to use horses for the task only came when yet another act was passed in 1783. Perhaps in the initial stages it was a combination of both. Indeed the Government turned something of a blind eye to the unofficial use of horsepower at the time.

The Official Opening of the Erewash Canal took place on 10 December 1779. Brightly decorated narrowboats with canal company shareholders and local dignitaries on board travelled the length of the canal in a colourful regatta. The occasion was deemed to have been 'a local triumph'. At Langley Bridge, the termination point, dignitaries, engineers, shareholders and their families – alongside those many hard-working navvies – fell in line behind garlands, buntings and a brass band. They were then taken to the place where a celebration dinner awaited them.

In May 1780 John Varley, at the age of forty, was sacked by the Erewash Canal Company. The reason given for his dismissal was the shareholders' dissatisfaction with the accounts he had periodically put before them. There were suggestions – perhaps allegations – that Varley had been embezzling funds, and while his engineering skills mainly satisfied the shareholders there had been problems. The company had recently been forced to take down a lock chamber which – using most of the same bricks – had had to be rebuilt.

Damage, still unspecified at this time, was blamed on the canal and its builders, and compensation payments were made accordingly, hence the shareholders' decision to sack John Varley. They maintained that the overall laying-out of the waterway should have been performed more smoothly and with little or no financial loss or pay-outs. However, the shareholding majority still considered Varley to be a fine engineer.

After 1790 the canal could truly be described as operational. Boats containing cargoes of bricks, lime, limestone, iron and coal were leaving the various wharves and travelling through the pounds of the Erewash Valley. Some boats returned empty with the boatsman ready to unload the next consignment and others journeyed in with returned goods.

By 1783 the demand for coal had heightened and the Erewash Canal Company approached the colliery owners. As new shafts were sunk, the company advertised their readiness to widen the marketing field for all parties concerned, the relative proximity of the Erewash Canal providing a good opportunity to distribute the coal. Nonetheless, there were still transportation problems to be overcome in the direction of the thriving Shipley coalfields.

It was decided to add further sections and branches to the Erewash Canal, and in 1789 the necessary Act was passed by Parliament; it included the coalfields around Pinxton in a proposed northern arm which would meet the Erewash Canal at Langley Bridge. This waterway, known as the Cromford Canal, provided perfectly adequate transportation for consignments of cotton from the Richard Arkwright Mills along with lime, lead, iron, bricks and coal.

Acts were then passed in 1793 authorising the building of the Nutbrook Canal. Its construction would considerably ease the Shipley coalfields and the Derby Canal's transportation problems and thus reassure shareholders as to the stability of their investment. The Derby Canal, extending for seventeen miles, left the Erewash Canal at Sandiacre and continued west through Breaston to White Bear Lock in Derby. The lock was named after the local public house, which was no doubt used frequently by navvies and boatmen alike! From there the water entered the Derwent Basin; the canal itself continued its journey beyond Peggs Flood Lock and turned southwards to meet the Trent & Mersey Canal.

By the time this waterway network had been completed all the branches were busy with boats and the canal companies, particularly at the Erewash, received a regular income from the tolls. The dividends paid to the shareholders of the Erewash Canal Company in these 'canal boom' years – 1791 to 1808 – fluctuated between 20 per cent and 30 per cent. In 1809 a dividend of 33.3 per cent was paid. In 1826 the shareholders were understandably delighted to be receiving 74 per cent. However, by 1856 a dividend of a 'mere' 20.7 per cent was agreed upon; this decrease in the dividend was mainly caused by the railway companies' rapid expansion and, in most parts, their virtual monopolisation of the transportation scene.

Back in the 1830s most colliery owners objected to what they considered to be the 'high tolls' charged by the canal companies, and the Erewash Canal Company was no exception. Rather than lose business the shareholders lowered their tolls accordingly. There was, after all, the threat of the colliery companies amalgamating. Such an amalgamation would have the financial resources to rival their position and, the necessary Acts of Parliament permitting, could well build a canal for the transportation of coal, and later perhaps iron and cotton. In view of this impasse the tolls were lowered and remained so. There was a further threat: the railways and the spreading network against which the canal companies realised they could barely compete.

Nevertheless, the share dividends still appeared progressive, with 11.3 per cent registering among the returns of 1871. Just thirty years later the Erewash Canal, in common with most of the Midlands canals, faced the threat of obsolescence. Industrial transportation was scant and there was no doubting that it was the railway companies that had put them out of business.

In 1932, following extensive business surveys, the Erewash Canal was taken over by the Grand Union Canal Company. Their intention was to control the entire canal network, extending from and around the Derbyshire coalfields to the wharves of London. This company, while

A boat with consignment in bygone times. (Courtesy of The Steamboat Inn)

recognising the threat of the railways, offered forms of transportation that, although slower, were undoubtedly cheaper. There was, the shareholders insisted, still a market for transporting coal and iron by canal, but this belief persisted for only a relatively short time.

Coal was still being transported down the Erewash Canal during the Second World War. Other consignments of goods were more unusual in that they had a direct link with the war effort. These consignments, made by the thousands of employees at Stanton Ironworks, were bomb cases destined for ammunition depots throughout the Midlands and others in London. On reaching the ammunition depots, the bomb cases were filled with the deadly explosives. When the war ended most canals, the Erewash included, faced an uncertain future. To this the new Labour Government responded by nationalising transport. This made the Erewash Canal unmanageable, its fate now to be decided by the British Transport Commission.

My late friend and doyen of the waterways, Ike Argeant, assured me that the last narrowboat transporting an unrecorded cargo down to the Erewash Canal passed through the lock gates in 1952. Ike, himself a professional waterman, used the waterway around his Sawley/Sandiacre homes and in 1954 was photographed at Padmoor Moorings, by the Nottingham–Derby Road Bridge.

In 1962 the Erewash Canal was officially declared unnavigable from Gallows Inn, Ilkeston, to the Langley Mill Basin, formerly Langley Bridge. However, local weekend pleasure boaters chose to ignore the declaration and continued making the journey from Trent Lock to Langley Mill, or to self-elected moorings below it if they chose. In fact, when the Transport Act of 1968 extended the official canal closure from Gallows Inn to Long Eaton, the boaters still made use of the waterway which, unlike the Nutbrook, remained in good repair.

In 1970 I was introduced to Joe, a Beeston resident who was also a canal enthusiast. Freshly retired, Joe bought a pleasure boat and regularly journeyed along the Erewash and Chesterfield canals, places which he described as being:

A bygone scene on the Erewash Canal. (Courtesy of Ike Argeant)

… absolute havens because you can go along for two or three days and not see a soul.

Nor did he meet with any forms of officialdom, adding gleefully:

I don't know whether I'm trespassing or not. All I know is that I'm really enjoying myself,

During its term of official disuse the Erewash Canal – in its wharves, winding holes and works barge turning points – nurtured such naturally colonising plants as the varied willows, alders, reed, sedge and water's edge sycamore. When I walked the towpath from Langley Mill to Cotmanhay in the 1970s I photographed, on the Derbyshire side, two work boats or barges; they were rotted and partially sunken but remained discernible in shape. Covered by reed and flowering yellow irises they were being used as a nesting and preening site by a family of moorhens.

In 1983/84 the Erewash Borough Council included the canal in its well-planned environmental scheme, which also involved the designation of three conservation areas within walking distance of Long Eaton, Sandiacre, and Ilkeston in particular. Thus the towpath was resurfaced, trees and shrubs were planted along the banks and towpath and seats were provided, along with explanatory notices at interesting and appropriate sites.

The Erewash Canal today is well used by leisure craft and narrowboat enthusiasts. Few are the summer evenings when one fails to see narrowboats passing through the lock at Gallows Inn, Ilkeston, where a corner of the pub interior then displayed paintings of narrowboats and local canal scenes. Each was a reminder that there is much to see in both directions and a world to explore just by stepping out on to that historic and much-used towpath.

Pleasure boating in the 1950s.

CHAPTER TWO

THE PEOPLE OF THE PAST

Historians have understandably focused much of their attention on establishing exactly when a particular canal course was started and finished. The recording of shareholders' accounts has also been closely scrutinised and yet despite this there is relatively little material available on the men who actually dug their spades into the ground. They dug day after day, week after week, as their unwritten job descriptions – and perhaps ambiguously worded contracts – demanded.

These men came to be known as 'navvies'; the name navvy is used to describe anyone involved in the task of excavating, whether of a quasi-singular or collective nature. Roads, canal beds and railway cuttings were dug out by these labourers, who exchanged their time and effort for what they hoped would be a fair wage.

But who were these men? From where did they originate to form gangs who could excavate a tract of land of 11¾ miles – in the case of the Erewash Canal – into a series of long pounds divided by lock gates, within the space of twenty months? I was once told that most navvies were Irishmen, and I lived with this belief until I met a painter at Stoke Bruerne Waterways Museum, near Daventry in Northamptonshire. As a boy he was told that navvies and the eventual owners of wide and narrow boats originated from gypsy stock. We agreed that a few may have been Irishmen and a few gypsies, while some were probably self-elected itinerants. But surely, we concluded, the majority would have been local men who preferred working out of doors rather than in the mills or down the mines? We developed the theory that the majority were local drifters who embarked on various labouring forms of employment as and when they became available.

A few of the navvies were likely to have been petty criminals, habitual drunkards, bullies and poachers. Along the route there would have been hirings and firings, but how many navvies the Erewash Canal Company employed at any particular time within those twenty historic months no one today can say for certain. But they were valued, for without the navvies there could have been no canal. Men of this type work hard and drink hard. Fist fights must have broken out in the living camps. I occasionally imagine approaching a still dry canal bed being worked by a team of navvies; there would undoubtedly have been an aggressive atmosphere, regardless of the weather. There would have been men wielding spades, picks and shovels. Bricklayers, joiners and painters would have been working on the lock gates. The scene would surely have resembled those depicted by the big screen, where teams of Chinamen are portrayed hewing the course of a railroad through the then recently chartered tracts of the American West. Several such Westerns were made in the 1970s and each in its way takes us

How the navvies preferred to see their rabbits.

back to the times when canals, roads, and eventually railways were similarly integrated with the existing landscape of Great Britain.

Where did these men sleep? I would think in elongated tents. Where did they eat? I would say from similarly shaped tables. I doubt that they were adequately fed, certainly when the tasks put before them are considered, therefore orchards and potato fields were undoubtedly plundered and game, particularly hares and pheasants, were poached with regularity.

THE BOAT PEOPLE

The first generations of boat people had to make crucial decisions on whether making a living from the waterways was really viable. Their occupation, like their boats, was not inherited. They were the pioneers and had only their own intuitions to follow. Eventually they would exchange the knowledge they had gained with their waterway peers and colleagues, boatmen, lengthmen and lock-keepers, and their shared experience strengthened them all.

But again one has to ask: from where did this generation originate? My Stoke Bruerne contact suggested that they developed from the navvies, who perhaps had married and found themselves seeking a challenge which would give them security once they had mastered the skills of transportation. This idea seemed reasonable. I then added that perhaps the younger generation of local millers and farmers, blacksmiths and farriers may also have been tempted by the chance of changing occupations. From whichever source or background these first generation boat people came, one thing was for certain: there was no shortage of them, either boat people or boats.

A small number set themselves up as boat builders and boat repairmen, all professions necessary for the smooth running of the Erewash or any other waterway company. To imagine that these boat people led the idyllic lives often depicted in watercolour paintings on display in garden centres, is, when taking into consideration the many and frequent hazards of the trade, way off the mark. There must have been certain halcyon days and, for the towpath walker, some unspoiled, picturesque scenery, but it should be remembered that by and large a waterman or woman was faced with a hard life. Regardless of rain, fog, blizzard and snow they still had to continue their journeys and get the boats through the lock gates as best and fast as they could. Sometimes it was possible for boats to go through certain locks two at a time. As they travelled they would, I imagine, have worried about how long they would have to wait before being unloaded or loaded at the wharves.

Waiting time, as it was called, became a bone of contention amongst the boat people. Fathers fell out with sons, there were repeated altercations with other families, and there were accusations of favouritism when it came to the better paid consignments. Tempers flared and fists were raised; mostly amongst the men, but sometimes amongst the women.

All the angst, the threats and quarrels were observed by the lock-keepers and their families. To some extent the 11¾ miles of the Erewash Canal would have taken on the appearance of a particularly elongated factory, just with invariably angry employees attempting to cajole their fellows into following their own wishes.

At the lock gates, camps and pubs – usually the day's destination – men played cards, or gambled. Skittles were always on hand in the camps, along with dominoes and darts. Friendships were made and promises broken, as is the case today in every community. There were decent families on the water, but often families were made up of troublemakers and scoundrels, something that was especially true during the early years. There was a time when waiting time payments were withdrawn by some wharfside companies; however, they were reinstated once the companies realised that the narrow boatmen were boycotting their consignments and choosing only the 'journeys that paid'. In winter, whenever ice formed overnight on the canal surface, 'ice breaker' boats made their appearance. These were described to me as being steel barges, each of which was manned by a maintenance crew of six men whose job it was to rock the boat from side to side and so break up the ice and create a channel along which the narrowboats could pass relatively unhindered.

The people in the local towns – like Long Eaton, Sandiacre and Ilkeston – who benefitted most during a 'freeze up' were the ice-cream sellers. After the ice layers had been broken up by the boats these men would use poles with hooks on the end with which they eased large chunks of ice over to the canal bank; they then lifted the chunks out with their gloved hands and placed them in tubs brought there on a handcar or wheelbarrow. The ice cubes were then wheeled to the ice-cream man's home or business premises, where they were stored in readiness for packing into ice boxes or meat safes. The ice was later transferred to a box holding quantities of iced lollies, the intention being to keep them in good condition for their sale from a boxed bicycle along the town and suburban roads.

WATERWAY OCCUPATIONS

Bricklayers and lock repairmen were probably employed at Trent Lock and Langley Mill. When not engaged in repair work they would assist the boat and barge repairmen. There would be a blacksmith and farrier's shop nearby with a boy apprentice engaged at each. A blacksmithing apprenticeship lasted four years.

A narrowboat matriarch. Some of the older women in this era are known to have regularly smoked pipes of tobacco. (Courtesy of The Steamboat Inn)

Prince the horse in 1930 beside two gravel boats, *Elm* and *Ash*, which were steered by the capable hands of Herbert, Ethel, Percy and Rowley. (Courtesy of Ike Argeant)

There were also stable boys working at and around the depots. Perhaps they envied those men who travelled out on the boats to do repairwork for their resentment was occasionally reported by a lengthman. Each lengthman worked a three-mile stretch of canal. They walked or cycled it daily to look for leaks before engaging in tasks like hedging and ditching. This care kept the towpath free from encroaching vegetation. A lengthman, if he lived in a waterway company property, would have kept his tools there. If not, then the company usually had a lock-up cabin built for him, which would be positioned beside the towpath and from where he would venture with billhook and mattock most days.

The maintenance team regularly had to fetch clay from the fields and pile it into the maintenance boat. This clay, known locally as 'puddlin' clay', was used for blocking up cracks or seams when they appeared in the canal bed. Having learnt from the lengthman that a particular stretch of waterway appeared to be leaking, the team would set out in the maintenance boat – they would only find the leak by prodding the canal bed with poles.

When the leak was discovered – which was indicated by continually swirling water – puddlin' clay was shovelled out of the boat to fill in the crack. This would usually be done by a junior employee, wearing waders and climbing feet first out of the boat then turning, all the while holding on to the sides of the boat with both hands. He would begin stamping repeatedly into the clay so that it spread, often quite unevenly, over the leake.

Then the maintenance foreman was satisfied the junior would be half-hauled back into the boat. 'Loll' Baker, whom I met a few years before he died, remembered the 'puddlin' days' with nostalgic affection:

After the job was done, we used to moor the boat and sit having our 'snap', our cheese sandwiches and flasks of tea, in the warm sunshine with nothing but the occasional lowing of cattle and always the singing skylarks to disturb the silence.

Of course, he was speaking about the 1920s and early '30s. He went on:

And it was lovely to sit biting into your cheese sandwiches and hearing the corncrakes calling when you were out Ilkeston and Cossall way. Sometimes we'd go looking for their eggs in the cornfields…

Stretches of canal bank, and occasionally the moorings, had to be made serviceable by these waterway repair teams. However, 'Loll' Baker told me that 'the morale was high amongst us even though we were poorly paid. And they were the days I would go back to if I had my time to come over again.' A veteran of the Erewash Canal Preservation Association told me that there was once a lock-keeper's house beside every set of lock gates along the Erewash Canal.

South of Ilkeston the locks appear to be named according to the location: Long Eaton, Dockholme, Sandiacre, Pastures, Hallam Fields and Gallows Inn. Beyond Gallows Inn the names no longer seem so specific: Greens, Potters, Barkers, Stensons before they revert back to location at Shipley Lock.

The Barkers, the family after whom one lock is named, are believed to have been the landowners who sold their twelve or so miles of land to the Erewash Canal Company, from where it passed on to other companies not directly associated with the canal. Perhaps this is the reason why the name also arises at Long Eaton, with the tract of water called Barkers Pond now accessible from Fields Farm Road?

Each of the canal companies employed clerks to keep the day books in order. This entailed recording every consignment of goods that a narrow boatman delivered to other destinations.

In quite beautiful handwriting, the clerks recorded the destination, the estimated weight of the consignment, the day it left the wharf, by which boat and finally when it arrived at its destination. The details of the latter were, of course, filled in several days later. Waiting times and toll fees were also recorded, by either the narrowboat men or a clerk.

A similar day book for toll fees was maintained at the toll payment point, which in the instance of the Erewash Canal was situated adjacent to The Lock House at Trent Lock, or 'Watersmeet' as it was known in those early days.

CHAPTER THREE

THE CANAL BOATS
AND HORSES

Judging by photographs one occasionally comes across depicting a canal or towpath horse, the average animal was not outstandingly sturdy, at least not in the sense of plough horses like the Shire and Clydesdale. However, the canal folk of times past may well have chosen to take me to task on these observations. In most of the photographs I have seen the animals appear to be the drey horse type. I am of the opinion that these horses were bought from fairs, markets and local farmers. According to an old boatman of the 1950s they were 'Nags in every sense of the word.'

However, there must have been narrowboat families who bought sturdy horses solely to tow the thirty-ton consignments of coal, iron, oil and housebricks from the various wharves. Their strength would surely be adequate recompense for the extra cost. A horse standing at seventeen hands was considered high for a canal horse. It had, after all, to go beneath the bridges. That being the case, horses of fourteen or fifteen hands (or less) were sought out. The majority of horse buyers connected to the waterways knew that the narrowboat companies and narrowboat men preferred mongrel stock. In their parlance they were described in singular fashion as 'a half-legged horse'. Most of the horses were owned by the canal companies and fewer were controlled by the narrowboat families themselves. There were also local suppliers, keen not just to sell the horses but to hire them out as well.

Stabling provided by the canal companies was to be found at most of the wharves and depots as well as local pubs. Shire horses were occasionally to be seen working around Trent Lock, probably due to the pulling power which was needed to get boats through the shallows prior to the building of the Sawley and Cranfleet cuts. They may have been used for haulage work involving lock gate repairs and such, but it was usually the mongrel horses which were to be seen on the canal towpath.

A single horse could move at around 2mph when it was pulling a loaded boat. If it was pulling heavily loaded narrowboats, as was sometimes the case, the speed was understandably reduced to around 1½mph. On a return journey, often with an empty boat, the speed picked up to an estimated 3¾mph. Horses, along with carts or wagons, were often waiting at the wharves to take the goods unloaded from the narrowboats to their respective destinations. The children of a narrowboat family often walked close behind or alongside the towpath horse to keep it travelling.

When my mother, living near the Nottingham Canal during her childhood, saw horses towing the narrowboats beneath the bridge or to the lock gates she used to run home and beg sugar lumps and carrots with which to feed them, 'and they always looked hungry those poor horses. Hungry and moth-eaten the lot of them,' she recalled. The same was probably

Canal horses and a stable hand, Barkers Lock, 1900. (Courtesy of Ike Argeant)

true of any waterway location. In most cases I get the impression that the average boatman, if faced with people offering sugar lumps and carrots, allowed his charge to snack briefly along the way.

At the Lock House Tearooms (situated on the Trent Lock) the model of a horse's head is affixed to an alcove wall. The model depicts the type of tack or harness worn by a towpath horse, including the once all-important 'blinkers'. Beneath this feature is a notice explaining that a boatman, or any other employee for that matter, could be sacked if they were caught riding a horse at the same time that it was pulling or hauling a load boat. Many boatmen looked upon their horses with a great deal of affection, to the extent of them almost becoming members of the family.

The late Ike Argeant, who in 1926/27 was living at Sawley (about half a mile from the Erewash Canal), told me once how at the age of sixteen he secured a living for himself as a boatman on the Grand Union Canal. His employer was the Trent Navigation Company. Ike's usual run was to Loughborough and Leicester; when he had delivered a consignment of goods he would ride the horse, in all weathers, back to Sawley or Nottingham. With great fondness he recalled that if he put the horse on the A46 he could fall asleep on its back, and wake as he was being guided into the stables at Wilford Street in Nottingham. If, on the other hand, he fell asleep after putting his charge on to the A6, he would wake up at the Argeants' house in Sawley. It was just a matter of putting the horse onto the road Ike required, then letting it do the rest.

'Tommy' was the most commonly used name for towpath horses in the locality. Besides walking the roads from Leicester to Nottingham, often unguided but with their son asleep on its back, the Argeants' Tommy would walk into the house if someone left the door open. He would then make for the table which he would clear of its mealtime contents, either by sampling from each plate or dish or pulling at the tablecloth. Roaring with laughter, Ike further recalled how many times someone had to pick up the food-laden table when Tommy came in. With their backs to the horse, they would turn the table from Tommy's investigative muzzle while shouting for another family member to come quickly and back the horse out into the yard.

I liked Ike's account concerning a narrowboat man called Tommy. Tommy cycled the towpath home after delivering a consignment to the Langley Mill Basin with his horse Dolly, her muzzle almost to Tommy's collar, trotting behind. Home to them both was a house and stabling close to Trent Lock. Their next journey may have begun a day or so later.

Where and when it was possible the summer grasses were allowed to grow tall on the hedgerow side of the towpath. They were then scythed down as a proportion of the canal company's hay harvest around August or September. Larger quantities of hay were delivered to the stable yards by either the local farmers or the horse feed and tack companies who, of course, welcomed the additional income.

Horses were most commonly seen towing the narrowboats. However, donkeys, mules and occasionally ponies were not unknown, particularly when additional transportation was needed around the wharves.

The Boats

From the plaques in the boating museums one learns that the early boats were iron-framed and filled in with timber planks, usually of oak. Wood was used with most boat builders and canal companies until steam power became predominant in the nineteenth century. In order to create the curves used for the stern and bows of each boat the planks were made pliable by arranging them in steam chests after which, to get them into the required curved positions, three or four men were needed along with perhaps a boy apprentice. This was obviously back-breaking work, but it gave great satisfaction when the task was eventually completed. The stern and bow of a boat promised each company a future, while the streamlined beauty of the design, which many of us still take for granted, had a great effect on workers' morale.

The bottom of a boat was usually built from elm. At the time working boats on the canals were the only boats on the canal; indeed they were the only type for which there was room. The boats were the traditional 70ft x 7ft 'narrowboat' type with a cabin at the back. The original cabins were usually of quite crude design and were used only as a place for a boatman to shelter or sleep.

While the average cabin was usually bereft of adornments on the interior, an art form by way of boat decorations on the exterior was eventually developed, probably because it was required that company identification be clearly displayed. Moreover, it was beneficial for all concerned if the name of the company and/or town met the eye of the people using the waterway. The company men were advertising the availability and proximity of wares to all concerned.

Boat decoration became a unique craft, and the boats' exteriors were usually painted when they were in dry dock for repairs. They look splendid even today. Boats are decorated with castle or roses designs, kindling or little troughs of flowers are affixed to the cabin roofs of many, and several have a bicycle strapped on or near the hatch.

Posing with a tarpaulined consignment. (Courtesy of The Steamboat Inn)

External boat decoration and painting is maintained to this day, occasionally by an artist and maybe a pupil or two who happen to be on board the boat. There is, it is good to know, also a Guild of Waterway Artists; these are people who strive to maintain high standards of pictorial design and are keen to both prevent the craft from foundering and to provide a tribute to those early pioneers.

The Canal Acts of 1884 and 1887 advised that since many boatmen were marrying and raising families a cabin could, or should, be installed at the front of the boat to serve as a children's bedroom. The wives, understandably, had a lot to do with the external and internal decorations of the boats although, weather permitting, some meals would be taken in picnic fashion out of doors and such chores as washing clothes had to be undertaken at the various moorings along the way. At night the newly added cabin could provide shelter for the entire family, even though it was just 6ft wide by 8½ft long. Most of the company boat owners begrudged this use of space as it had previously been used for cargo shipment. In most cases they were conveying less cargo but more people. But the larger cabin remained.

The standard living cabin of a narrowboat contained a stove, a table that folded down from the wall and similarly a fold-down bed. An in-built cupboard or two and a drawer unit on either side were usually enhanced by an imitation wood grain design which was splendidly decorated with coloured ribbons and lace plates. In the winter could there be a cosier situation? Come the hot nights of the summer some family members would even sleep rolled in a sheet beside the towpath hedgerow or on a nearby embankment.

Early engines were offered to the various canal companies to break the narrowboats dependency on horsepower, but none proved satisfactory. Steam engine tugs were seen towing boats along the rivers, but few, if any, were seen on the canals. In the 1870s the steam engine took hold. Canal company men had them fitted to both narrowboats and wideboats. They also proved beneficial in towing a second boat, usually unpowered and called a 'butty'. But it was not until the recognised 'steam days' of the early twentieth century that the steam–driven boat replaced horse towing, and even then the change was not universal.

The pay of a boatman and his family was deemed adequate by the authorities. The experiences of the boatmen suggested otherwise; consequently some boatmen stopped working for the companies and, having acquired contracts along the way, set up their own businesses, thereby competing directly with their former employers.

CHAPTER FOUR

AROUND TRENT LOCK

From the suggestions of a settlement at Clifton – evidence of a trough and cooking facilities in a Willington quarry and a Bronze Age log boat having been unearthed at Shardlow – we can infer that Bronze Age man at some stage explored the river banks around Sawley and Red Cliff, even if it was only as a hunter.

A short walk upstream of Trent Lock brings the spire of Sawley church into view. Somewhere around here a Roman road once linked Ryknield Street to the Fosse Way. Much evidence of Roman occupation has been found along the Trent, particularly on the meandering downstream stretch to Attenborough. Therefore it would not be unreasonable to suggest that, bank erosion and flood scheme projects apart, there have been people of a variety of cultures exploring the banks of the Trent since time immemorial.

A ferry linked the south banks of the Trent with Sawley church, which it is thought was first used by the Saxons. Then, around 1500, a causeway and stone bridge was built and maintained until the late eighteenth century. This was later replaced by an iron bridge in the early nineteenth century. Monks journeyed the riverside and spread the word of Christianity from the sixth or seventh-century monastery at Repton: this is how the church opposite the already well-established crossing place at Sawley was founded. In the ninth century it came to be listed under the holdings of the See of Lichfield.

Sawley church was fitted with chancel arches in Norman times. In all probability the stonework for the church was transported by river boat, in a similar manner to the Normans making use of the Roman-built Fossdyke when transporting the stones used for building Lincoln Cathedral. The banks of the Trent in this area have always been busy and innovatively used.

The arrival of canal company engineers in the seventeenth century, and later on the supervised teams of navvies, had little to do with food supply or religion. Rather it was chiefly concerned with this new form of transportation and the wealth that could be gained from it. 'Watersmeet' was clearly a place of ongoing activity: lock builders and repairmen, boat builders and repairmen, teams of navvies, all were busily engaged with their labours. Their work would eventually result in the arrival of narrowboats, boatmen and their families, The stables and the related occupations, from blacksmith to horse boy, would follow later, especially after 1783.

There were people travelling and people logging the journeys while others worked paying and collecting the tolls. Boatmen, boat builders, farriers, ferrymen, loaders and unloaders worked every day, in almost every hour of daylight and often in adverse weather conditions. That was the scene at Watersmeet – or Trent Lock, as it came to be known – towards the end of the eighteenth century, a time of profound change in Britain.

Canal-boat families, Trent Lock. (Courtesy of Ike Argeant)

For the Erewash Canal Company, the most important concern – aside from the wharf offices where the day books were filled in – was undoubtedly the lock house where the tolls had to be paid. Built in 1794, probably to replace a duty person who may have originally operated from a shed or shelter beside the lock, the lock house was equipped with a rear yard stable and blacksmithing facilities. There is still an extensive orchard today; this is where poultry and goats were once kept. From an informative colour leaflet, produced by the Ashby family who now reside at the cottage and run the Tea Rooms, one learns that the lock house has been modernised over the years in keeping with the requirements of the obvious succession of lock-keeping residences. In the present-day cellar there is evidence of fly boat crews having resided there. Alongside the sleeping quarters was a brick and iron coal fire, mainly used to heat water, and also a kitchen range.

A small room, redolent of a prison cell, was then discovered; presumably it had been used for confining known thieves and undesirables. Perhaps drunkards were also put in the cell for an overnight stay – or maybe even longer – and also the occasional hothead who was keen to fight either beside or around the lock, or in the bar of The Steamboat next door. As the Ashbys, through their own personal research, have pointed out, some form of law and order was obviously established at Watersmeet in those times.

Adjacent to the lock house is the toll house. Here the tolls were paid, presumably before the keeper opened the lock gates. Alongside the lock stands The Steamboat, built in 1791. Like most pubs dating from those times The Steamboat has undergone several changes. Its patrons in those times must have been colourful people in every sense of the word. Skittles, dominoes and darts evenings would have been staged regularly. Sing-songs around a piano were looked forward to and social events would have been a local highlight, especially during and between the wars. I should add that in those days The Steamboat was called The Erewash Navigation. Photographs taken in the 1920s and '30s show that it was then named The Fisherman's Rest. Sitting in The Steamboat today with a pint of mild or a cup of coffee before me, I realised while watching the pleasure boat people negotiating the lock gates that the hardstanding alongside was probably the place where the aforementioned troublemakers and hotheads chose to settle their differences.

The varied buildings were, and some still are, storehouses for waterways equipment, the large British Waterways building having been completed in 1950. Crossing the lock bridge directly opposite The Lock House, one meets with the small pump house partially surrounded by a low hawthorn hedge. In the company of friends I have passed the narrow upright type building without realising that it was, and perhaps still is, very much a part of the Trent Lock scene. Pump houses were built with the intention of providing water reasonably quickly when extra water along the route was needed. Even canals with feeder reservoirs were equipped with pump houses; their used depended on the amount of boats using a particular waterway. The water was pumped by steam. Since the 1990s electric pumps have been used.

A narrowboat moored below Trent Lock. The cluster of cottages comprised the ferryman's house, canal company work and repair shops. The inn, perhaps then The Fisherman's Rest, is to the right alongside the lock house with toll payment office alongside. (Courtesy of Mike Taylor, *The River Trent Navigation*, 2000)

A busy riverside in the early 1900s. The ferryman is working the passenger ferry with the horse ferry lying unused in the foreground. An interesting boat, an Upper Trent lighter, is moored beside the narrowboats. (Courtesy of Mike Taylor, *The River Trent Navigation*, 2000)

The Navigation Inn.

The Steamboat Inn.

Just on from the pump house is The Navigation Inn which was, like many pubs in England, built to house a farming family. Presumably they grazed their stock on what is now the golf course complex, with the animals could wandering the length of Lock Lane. The farm itself was built in the eighteenth century. The outside notice informs the visitor that it was converted to a public house 'between 1910 and 1920'. It is a sizeable, low-beamed establishment and one can imagine both farming and publican families living here.

Both The Trent Navigation and The Steamboat brought valued trade to the waterside settlement; when the two pubs were being built a larger number and greater variety of craftsmen intermingled than had ever been the case before. Diverging at the point where the Lock House orchard merges with the hedgerow fields, the Cranfleet Cut takes boaters, intending to remain on the Trent, by the shallows between Radcliffe and Thrumpton to the lock and lock-keeper's house. The lock-keeper's house is situated above the river, which proceeds to meander in the direction of nearby Attenborough in Nottinghamshire, with Beeston and the city of Nottingham beyond.

Before Cranfleet was cut in 1797 boats had to be winched through the shallows and dredged by a gravel plough; they would be pulled by a horse or horses and this operation had to be undertaken almost daily to guarantee a relatively safe passage. Upstream, and within sight of Sawley church, another channel was cut in 1795 to bypass the shallows there. A lock and lock house were also built, the tolls for which would have been collected at Sawley.

CHAPTER FIVE

WITHIN LIVING MEMORY

Among the people who lived around Trent Lock in the early 1930s was Alan Heath of Long Eaton. Alan spent his formative years on a houseboat called *Alfresco*. The *Alfresco* was moored on the last part of the bend by the Mills Dockyard field, and within sight of the lock and its outbuildings. Alan, the son of Grace and George Heath, remembers his father going to and from work by boat in 1932 due to the winter floods of that year.

Their houseboat neighbours were William and Doris Lewis, who kept a houseboat pet, a cat called Pompy. William worked for the railway until Doris died when, understandably, he left the houseboat and took a house in Sawley (or Long Eaton).

Another houseboat couple were Mr and Mrs Rivers. Mr Rivers was a painter and decorator, his wife a tutor in shorthand who typed at the Long Eaton Business College.

Two or three cottages were situated by the entrance to Mills Dockyard where it joins Lock Lane. The canal bridge was also close by to provide easy access. The cottages were likely to have been built to house canal company employees. One of the residents was Ted Smith, who married Lavinia Heath, sister of Jesse Heath, Alan's grandfather.

Alan remembers the bombings of the Second World War, and in particular the destruction of the ferryman's house that had been occupied by Joe Rice. Joe survived the bombing and continued to work as a ferryman until the early 1950s. His house was not rebuilt and so Alan assumes that Joe found alternative accommodation nearby.

Trent Lock and the red cliffs were targeted by German bombers on several occasions, presumably due to their proximity to the railway. In particular the bridge leading to Red Hill tunnel received special attention from the Luftwaffe. In Alan's time the imposing private residence with gates now facing The Navigation Inn was lived in by a Mr Wheway. Built around 1889, the house is not thought to have been associated with the waterways or any managerial/overseer's position related to them. On the site of the present-day golf course and centre Alan remembers the land during his boyhood being used as a fly ash tip which frequently caught fire due to ashes from the passing trains being discarded there.

Some dusky evenings the land tract would glow, and while the hot ash was smouldering there were no outward displays of concern. But once the flames were seen to be high and spreading then someone would send for – presumably by bike – the local fire brigade. Horses, carts and dreys were still very much in use around Trent Lock in the 1930s and narrowboats, each pulled by the towpath horse, passed daily with consignments of flour. Joe Rice, the ferryman, regularly rowed parties of weekend anglers across the Trent, after which they would cross the fields and settle in along the banks of the Soar. Joe's charge was threepence per person. In the evening he would be called from the opposite bank to bring them back.

There was a tubular gate blocking the river bank by Mr Wheway's house for many years. Consequently, one would imagine that the houseboat people of Trent Lock did not venture beyond it and walk to Sawley Lock, as they do today. From the canal towpath one could then look across the field to Fletchers Pond, as you can today, except that in the past there were fewer hawthorns screening the water. Alan cannot remember there being chalets along the fieldside; together we explored the possibility of them being put up as 'summer weekend houses' after the war. Presumably the chalet people paid a rent to the land agent or family involved with the running of nearby Fields Farm.

An unexploded First World War bomb was recovered by a local diving team on the bed of Fletchers Pond, while Alan recalls at least two bombs during the Second World War being dropped in the fields. These bombs had fallen just short of their intended target, again the railway. Fletchers Pond is believed to have been so named to commemorate a bygone angler who spent most of his free time and weekends there.

On both sides of the railway there are ponds known simply as railway ponds because they were dug out by railway company employees. The earth was used to build up the railway embankments that were a necessity when routes took the trains across marshy, low-lying land. Alan, like the author, has explored these ponds and small lakes, which were given names like Triangular Pond, Victoria Pond and Forbes Hole. This is now a well-recognised and important nature reserve; thanks are due to Alan and his present-day conservationist colleagues. Alan's passion for the canals and sure-footedness around them can perhaps be attributed to his childhood. Life as a toddler on the *Alfresco* brought Alan close to the swan family which came with their cygnets to the houseboats to be fed. Alan never once missed his footing and tumbled into the canal. There was a day, however, when his mother's wedding or engagement ring slipped from her finger and into the water. Standing nearby, her husband George knelt, put his arm directly down, scooped and pulled up a fistful of mud and weed in the midst of which gleamed the fugitive ring.

Due to Alan needing to be schooled in Long Eaton, the Heath family moved from the canal bank to 5 Brown's Road. However, Trent Lock had already given Alan a grounding in country life which gave him a great respect for the environment and instilled in him the need to conserve our natural resources. These are principles which still guide him to this day.

WATERWAYS PEOPLE: ISAAC ('IKE') ARGEANT

Although christened Isaac, the name 'Ike' stuck almost from the day he was born in 1921. Besides Ike, there were five brothers and sisters living at the house in Castle Street, Nottingham.

The house was situated close to the Fellows, Morton and Clayton Wharf on the Nottingham Canal, and although Ike's parents worked the waterways, they were also fairground people who owned a set of steam-driven galloping horses, two cakewalks and a rifle range.

Ike's earliest recollections of a canal and waterways travel are of an experience in 1924. The Argeants were on a working trip along the Grand Union Canal transporting a long forgotten consignment from Hemel Hempstead to Nottingham. While his parents steered the narrowboat through a set of lock gates, Ike began toddling in the grasses and exploring the willow thickets where eventually he sat and fell asleep. It was not until the family were several miles up the waterway that someone realised he was missing. The Argeants hastily secured the boat in the first available mooring. Then his mother detached the horse from the towing rope, swung onto the bank and rode back along the towpath. To her relief, Ike was still curled up asleep in the thickets

Right: Alan Heath and his father and houseboat in the background. (Courtesy of Alan Heath)

Below: George and Grace Heath on the Mills Dockyard bank. (Courtesy of Alan Heath)

A working day scene as Ike Argeant would have known it. (Courtesy of Ike Argeant)

and grasses beside the lock gates; on awakening he discovered that he was on his mother's lap as she rode the horse back to the boat.

As the Argeants began spending more time on the waterways than in the fairgrounds Ike, along with his brothers and sisters, attended the nearest school to wherever their narrowboat happened to be moored. Ike explained that sometimes the would spend a few days in Leicester and move to Loughborough before calling at Sawley. On the return they would spend the next fortnight at a school in the centre of Nottingham which was close to Ike's basic home. In those strictly tutorial classrooms the children were taught 'the three Rs': reading, writing and arithmetic. Ike's parents had been good scholars themselves and taught their children much more besides. The senior Argeants worked the narrowboats owned by the former Erewash Canal Company, and by the age of ten Ike described himself as having become, and been paid as, their horse boy.

Leafing through his early photographs in his genial company, I was fascinated to see prints depicting a horse being brought across the Trent. They were transported from the mouth of the Soar to Trent Lock in a ferryboat, with the men and horse boys standing on either side. Although most of the narrowboats by then transported house bricks and coal (and, by the 1920s, freshly milled flour), Ike's family used to transport tar for distillation from wharves in Loughborough, Leicester and Peterborough. Ike recalled the 'ice-breaker boats', as mentioned elsewhere, and added that sometimes the ice was so thick that if a layer of snow from the previous night provided footing, the horse could actually be walked over the frozen surface.

In such conditions a narrowboat family were fortunate if they could clock up four miles a day, and Ike told me himself of a time when it took seven days to travel seven miles. However, on such nights it was snug and warm in the boat cabin, provided the family had collected the fuel, but the problem was that if a narrowboat family was stuck between destinations there was no money to be earned and no readily available fuel. Recalling the better days, Ike mentioned the waiting time monies paid out by the companies if a narrowboat family was moored in a wharf and waiting to be unloaded. The waiting time payment for two boats, one towing 'a butty' perhaps, was ten shillings, while a single boat received five shillings over a forty-eight-hour period.

By 1926/27 the Argeants were living at Sawley 'close to the Trent'. At the age of sixteen Ike, wanting independence, secured a living for himself as a boatman on the by-then familiar Grand Union Canal. His employer was the Trent Navigation Company. As I have also mentioned in a former chapter, Ike worked with a horse called Tommy, whose tablecloth removing antics have also been related!.

Eventually Ike changed employers and became a gravel towboat driver working the beds of the Trent and its adjacent gravel extraction areas between Clifton and Colwick, which lay just to the east of Nottingham. There were plentiful numbers of herons and kingfishers in those times, the non-breeding swans and now-extinct corncrakes called from the fields, and Ike came to have a deep understanding of the area and its waterways.

The Trent was also home to a thriving population of salmon which attracted the otters, some pairs of which bred and established their 'holts' in the wooded cliff banks at Clifton and Redhill Lock, near the mouth of the Soar. This, Ike told me, was one place in particular where if you were working close to the riverside cliffs then you would regularly come across the remains of the salmon caught by otters; several litters of cubs must have seen their first light of day among the willows, alders and glacier-smoothened boulders and pebbles of Redhill.

I was reminded of this on one recent Easter Monday morning when I visited the Country Fair at Thrumpton Hall. Assuming the riverside meadows to be included in the price of a ticket for the estate, two friends and I wandered down to the shallows below the weir and saw the elongated spits of gravel where the local otters had devoured their freshly caught salmon some fifty or sixty years before. Although his working section of the Trent provided much in the way of wildlife, Ike yearned to see more of the waterways in general and so he was hired for a spell of work along the Black Country waterways by Fellows, Morton and Clayton.

The horse-drawn flyboat had, by this time, been superseded by a motor-driven craft. This was an entirely new experience for Ike, whose lifestyle certainly changed. Sometimes he was woken at four in the morning when an unloading team met his boat at the wharves. At Bayliss, Jones & Bayliss, Ike's cargo would consist of hardware including boxes of nails, nuts and bolts. At Dudley Port, 'Vono' bedspreads were loaded and taken to Birmingham where the holds of the boat were then stacked with roles of corrugated paper, thirty or forty rolls at a time.

Ike worked these Black Country routes until 1946, which was the year he met the lady 'boatman', or 'mate', who became his wife. Did Ike meet his wife, Ellen Saunders, at a dance? In a cinema? A pub perhaps? Not a bit of it! As we have come to expect of him, they met on the water.

Both Ellen and Ike were employed by the same company, Fellows, Morton and Clayton. Ike had moved onto the company's southern section routes linking Birmingham to London where he soon familiarised himself with the Regents Canal. Ellen, by contrast, was employed along the northern section which covered all the canal wharves from Birmingham to Manchester, including Ellesmere Port.

Ellen, being employed as a 'mate', was on the payroll, as were all the single women; but once they were married each was regarded as 'a narrow boatman's wife'. From then on, whether they worked alongside their husbands or not, they were deemed ineligible for any kind of payment.

Ike pleasure boating at Padmore Moorings 1954. (Courtesy of Ike Argeant)

One day Ellen had a close brush with death. She was one of a crew of four employed in the transportation of oil. Their boat ran aground on an island in the middle of the Trent between the Cranfleet Cut and Beeston. The island was underwater then, as it is today, but at the time there were no depth or shallows warning signs as there are today. In Ike's words, 'You either made it or you didn't.'

Like a number of people I was surprised by Ike's account of an island along that particular stretch of the Trent. Other than the well-known and quite conspicuous Barton Island that levels with the gravel extraction lakes of the Attenborough Reserve I know of very few. However, during the drought periods of 2003 and 2004, from the towpath near the mouth of the River Erewash I saw two swans preening on a series of hummocky mounds and decided that in all probability this was the low-level island from which Ike rescued Ellen, her crew mates and the consignment of oil.

The first Ike knew of the oil boat being stranded was when he returned home tired following a day's work and received a telephone call from his employers asking if he would take out a boat and attempt to recover the oil boat crew. Ike took out a cob boat to the submerged island, boarded the oil boat and found Ellen in the cabin with her three work mates. He successfully liberated all four in one of the most treacherous of English rivers.

Ike's wife Ellen was born to Benjamin and Betsy Saunders at Ellesmere Port on 27 February 1924. Because her parents were employed on the narrowboats, soon after leaving school Ellen became 'a mate' or 'boat girl'. When her mother remarried, Ellen began working for Fellows, Morton and Clayton. She then joined her uncle, George Theobald, and worked his horse-drawn narrowboats *The Gipping* and *Kubina*; Ellen experienced a narrow escape from the latter when it was decimated by a ship's prop.

The River Trent at Trent Lock, one of the
most treacherous rivers in England.

Ike could not forget Ellen and began to take a particular interest in transporting goods to
Ellesmere Port. He conversed with her whenever they met along the waterways, particularly
along the Shropshire Union Canal, a stretch of water for which he would develop a great
affection. By his own admission Ike soon had Ellen's trade routes mapped out. He knew what
days she was off or due into Wolverhampton and arranged his journeys accordingly. The couple
were married at Sawley church on 19 May 1945.

The year of Ike and Ellen's marriage was also the one in which Fellows, Morton and Clayton
contemplated selling out to the British Transport Commission. Ike, however, found employment
with the Trent Navigation Company as a dredger operator working the Trent between
Nottingham and Newark. This gave Ike quite a varied working life, mainly due to crane and steel
pile driving being included among his responsibilities. By this time Ike and Ellen were raising a
family. In their free time they travelled the waterways of the Black Country in between visiting
Ellen's family at Ellesmere Port.

Ike was in the lock-keeper's cottage, which is now used as the headquarters and interpretative
centre for the Erewash Canal Preservation Society. When I first met him, I was exploring the
footpaths linking the railway marshalling yards at Toton to the towpath of the Erewash Canal
between Long Eaton and Sandiacre with two friends. The early sunset was burning across the
water surface and, from the cottage, smoke was rising from the chimney just as it would have
been in the old days.

A sign outside welcomed visitors in, so that they could have a look round and learn something
about the waterways and the way of life of the people who lived on them. This is a lifestyle that
is now recorded in books, or on photographs and paintings, but much less frequently on film.
Once across the lock gates we received a warm welcome as we entered the lock cottage, several

members of the Preservation Association were busying themselves with various tasks around the fireside while they greeted us.

I had heard of Ike Argeant long before I met him, and when the man knitting a fender was introduced to me as Ike, I decided that there was surely only one Ike in the area. I was soon conversing with this warm, unassuming man, whose skills and knowledge earned him a continuous living from the waterways.

By this time members of the Erewash Canal Preservation and Development Association were serving sherry. We saw in the New Year together and then had a refill, or 'warmer' as our kindly hostess described it. Minutes later, and with the early darkness coming in, I had persuaded Ike to allow me to call on him later in the year and record something of his interesting life.

As Ike and I leafed through his numerous postcard and photograph albums featuring waterways, locks, lock houses and narrowboat families and gatherings at his home backing on to the Erewash Canal between Dockholme and Sandiacre Lock, it became apparent that he must have travelled through pretty well all the waterway sections in England and some in Wales. Ike's nod and smile confirmed this before he continued relating his last years on the waterways. By 1966 Ike had accepted the position of foreman for teams responsible for maintaining the lock gates, dredging operations and towpath trimming duties along the Cromford, Erewash, Nottingham and Grantham canals, all of which were by then lingering in a state of uncertainty as to their futures.

Ike was later employed as a lengthman-foreman along his close-to-home Erewash Canal and was awarded the Queen's Silver Jubilee Medal in 1977. At the time of my visit Ike was retired and had been widowed for five years but, he told me, he still journeyed by boat up to Ellesmere Port and quite often imagined Ellen to be waiting for him there.

Ike died, I believe, at the age of seventy-eight, as he was journeying by narrowboat along the Shropshire Union Canal to Ellesmere Port. My waterways informant described his sad passing: he had 'just gone through a lock gate. Then it came, the heart attack. And he collapsed and died on the towpath, just as we all knew he would have wanted.'

The funeral at Sawley church was memorable. His photograph albums were on display and as his coffin was brought into the church the chug-chugging of a boat engine could be heard in the background. The legendary leather belt that had barely left Ike's waistline for five years and known to all the members of his family, friends and work colleagues, was coiled on top of the coffin. Thus the Erewash Canal has lost the last of its great raconteurs and professional boatmen.

George Brown, a resident of Long Eaton, once recalled how he and his wife Jenny cycled down the towpath on hot summer Sunday afternoons in the 1940s, much like my girlfriend Val and I would a decade later. George remembered leaving two bicycles at Joe the ferryman's house and paying the 3d or 6d each return to Joe, who then rowed them across the Trent. Now carrying a picnic basket on the opposite bank, George and Jenny then threaded their way between grazing Dairy Shorthorn and Ayrshire cattle to the Sawley Cut and crossed Redhill Lock to reach the rowing boat sheds on the banks of the Soar, near Kegworth and Kingston. For another sixpence each they took out a rowing boat for an hour and just lazed alongside the willows and reedy banks of the river, while still keeping Red Hill in sight but viewing it from a different angle. The couple sometimes picnicked when they had the boat out, but more often when they were alone, 'except for the skylarks and cattle', in the water meadows. When, in the late dusks, Joe rowed them back to Trent Lock, they occasionally saw a barn owl hovering 'like a great white moth' along the riverbank beside the fly ash fields.

In the summer of 1956 the author recalls similar happy memories. Val and I would cycle from the Nottingham suburb of Aspley along the green shaded boulevard system to Beeston, then continue along the A453 through Long Eaton to the canal bridge on Tamworth Road. Here we diverted to the canal towpath, the fields of wheat and barley to the left, the mirrored canal and the varied houses and bungalows on the opposite bank to the right.

The Lock Cottages and Toll House, Sandiacre. There were two cottages, one occupied by the lock-keeper, one by the lengthman. Stables were also attached.

Rowing on the Soar.

The track was stony and we were always hoping that we would not get a puncture. What I now know to be Sheet Stores Basin appeared to be little more than a deserted boatyard to us, but it was a place where we paused to take in the midsummer carpets of yellow water lilies.

Beyond the railway bridge willows, alders and hawthorn lined the opposite bank. Here moorhen pairs had established territories and nests that could be seen protruding like small bulky islands within the reed stems. Over to the left cattle grazed on the fields. It was still the Dairy Shorthorn and Ayrshires in those times, and the chalets were established close to Fletchers Pond. Close to the Mills Dockyard, the local swan pair had a nest on the grass bank and hatched off six cygnets. The male – or cob – was an exceptionally heavy bird. Trees and houseboats on the opposite bank between the bridge and Trent Lock outbuildings created an H.E. Bates atmosphere of deep foliage and reflected tranquillity. Alan Heath, whom I was to meet in later years, had left with his parents twenty-one years before our sojourn. The cranes and other items of lifting and tackle equipment stood redundant and rusting by the outbuildings.

Passing The Steamboat and the lock, we headed for the towpath of the Cranfleet Cut and were therefore not aware of either the bombed site where Joe's cottage had stood, the pumping house or the house once lived in by Mr Wheway that faced the Trent. The Cranfleet waterway and towpath were, on each of our visits, deserted. We sunned ourselves and picnicked just beyond the railway bridge opposite a reedy basin that may once have been a winding hole.

Moving on in the early evening we bypassed the Cranfleet Lock gates and lock-keeper's cottage, which had a solitary narrowboat opposite. This was the home of a reclusive woman with long white hair who glared at us on the few occasions that we saw her and never answered our greetings. We assumed that she shopped by crossing the fields to Long Eaton and, in retrospect, New Tythe Street, of which we were unaware. We imagined her as wearing a long overcoat, Wellington boots and a wide-brimmed hat, squelching across the fields in the teeming rain or surrounded by an austere blanket of fog. She may well have collected her milk, and perhaps some fruit and vegetables, from the nearby farm. Reclusive or immobile townsfolk would often be visited by the local gamekeeper (in this case he would probably have come from the Thrumpton estate) and they would be given an occasional brace of pheasants or rabbits. They were seldom, if ever, left to go 'without'.

From the Cranfleet Lock we cycled along the winding riverbank path to Attenborough. Cattle again grazed the fields to our left, while today gravel extraction lakes enhance the scene. On one occasion a man cycling in the opposite direction stopped to have a word and, pointing to the spire of Attenborough church rising above the distant trees, told us that in our lifetimes the entire area from the Plessey Communications factory at Beeston to New Tythe Street, Long Eaton, would all be pretty well underwater. His prediction has proved correct. From Attenborough we continued along to Beeston Lock, then followed the canal towpath of the Nottingham Canal to Lenton and the boulevard system that unfortunately left the waterways and took us back to Aspley. On those Sunday cycle rides we at least learned how the waterways linked up and at the same time we explored the possibility of one day living on a houseboat or in a house with a front garden facing the canal, much like the one we saw at Canalside, Beeston.

THE 1960s

In the 1960s I was employed as a furniture salesman at Jays Furnishers on the corner of Regent Street. On the lunch hours that I was not escorting a pretty insurance clerk along the High Street pavements or around the Friday and Saturday market stalls, I took my sandwiches up to Long Eaton Lock.

Erewash Canal, Trent Lock, 1956, with cranes and jibs in the background.

What struck me then, unlike today, was the sense of desertion along the towpath. There were no pleasure boats and relatively few people. When I became a television rentals collector I rode my moped on fine sunlit Fridays along the towpath to Trent Lock, where again I ate my sandwiches beside the river. Here, as along the canal, there was a deep sense that the waterway had been deserted. I remember having the occasional pint of bitter in The Steamboat, but whether this popular hostelry was open every Friday lunchtime I cannot recall. There were certainly no other customers in during my visits, largely due to Friday having become the day when almost everyone visited the shops and the still relatively new supermarkets.

On my regular round from Stapleford to Sawley, which extended over a four-day period, the Trent or Erewash Canal was sometimes touched upon in conversation. Middle-aged women reminisced over walking from Sawley to work in the mills and factories. When the ice was hard and the ground layered with frozen snow they would link arms at the Tamworth Road bridge and walk on the surface of the canal, 'perhaps sometimes for an entire week of early mornings before the ice showed signs of melting.'

An early 1960s view of the area immediately beyond Trent Lock.

Some enthusiasts took their ice skates with them to work and similarly strapped them on when they reached the Tamworth Road Bridge. Ice skating was a weekend pastime for quite a few enthusiasts in the cold winters of the past. I have been told that people skated 'for miles' along the frozen canal surface. Others skated on the Farmers, Triangular and Fletchers ponds as well as Forbes Hole.

Floodings occurred annually, usually after a prolonged snowfall. I was told by a waterman that it took four days for water from melting snow to reach the Trent Valley after descending down the fissures of the Staffordshire and Derbyshire hills. In modern times, due to technological improvements the impact of melting snow (the last memorable surge occurred in the year 2000) is felt by the low-lying fields and lock houses only two to three days after a thaw has set in.

However, the flooding of the year 2000 could hardly be compared with those floods of the past. Most people living in the centre of Long Eaton had to take their furniture and live in the upper storeys of their homes. Firemen and various rescue teams transferred the elderly by rowing boat to alternative accommodation. The flood of 1947 had a particularly devsastating impact. The High Street was left underwater and shops closed.

Long Eaton Market Place sometimes flooded.

In the 1930s and '40s residents with 3–4ft of water later inundating their homes, such as became a regular occurrence in Charnwood Avenue and Mikado Road, were helped out or rescued by groups representing the Army Home Guard, Sea Scouts and Cadets. The Royal Air Force launched rubber dinghies on behalf of the Red Cross.

If the marooned residents chose not to leave their homes but instead moved their belongings upstairs, then the Red Cross and other helpers would regularly supply them with food. I was told that more than one bungalow-dwelling family was forced to scramble up to seek sanctuary in the rafters. Discussing the size of the floods in 1947, one householder showed me a newspaper cutting and photograph depicting Dr J.P. Denny leaving an Army lorry and preparing to be carried piggyback to the flooded houses of the sick and ailing. He emphasised:

Long Eaton market place was like a bloomin' great lake. It was paddle, paddle, paddle, in yer wellies wherever you went. There was no market of course. No shops open. No anything. It was all just water. And we all thought it would never go away…

High Street, Long Eaton, in the 1960s.

One group who did benefit were the local anglers. They recalled days spent 'fishing within five minutes walk of the front door'!

A couple living near The Hole In The Wall pub on Regent Street recalled some of the local narrowboat men frequenting that hostelry, particularly in the late 1930s and early '40s when they were transporting consignments of flour. The top of Regent Street terminated at the canal towpath, where the narrowboats were moored. The swan pair that nested annually in the reeds by the factory wall on the other side of the Derby Road bridge used to climb up the natural bank; when their cygnets were large enough to do the same then they would pad in file down the centre of the street, where residents used to feed them daily with bread.

I have gleaned stories of similar incidents concerning the Padmore Moorings stretch of canal at Sandiacre and the row of cottages or terraced houses, now demolished, that stood adjacent to The Gallows Inn, Ilkeston. The short street also terminated at the canal towpath near here, and the local swan pair and cygnets used to leave the waterway and waddle in file to the doors of the families who would habitually feed them.

During the 1960s, reed clumps and beds of yellow water lily enhanced the canal surface while at the same time an interest in pleasure boats or cabin cruiser life was increasing. Dinghies and fibre-glass cabin cruisers became popular and once again the boat builders were busy; old established premises were being revamped and new premises, boatyards and small marinas were opening up to meet what was described as the 'new boom in waterway traffic'.

A well-made and well-maintained cabin cruiser, boat builders insisted, could last eighty or ninety years and interested people – of which there were many – began exploring the capital outlay. The narrowboats were steel-hulled. Boats were designed and built specifically for use on the inland waterways. Lock gates were checked and where possible improved or repaired

Right: The Hole In The Wall, Regent Street, in the 1960s.

Below: Erewash Canal between Long Eaton and Dockholme Lock, in the 1960s.

Left: Erewash Canal between Tamworth Road and Sheet Stores Basin.

Below: The scene in 1964, looking along the Erewash Canal towpath towards Trent Lock.

and sluices were inspected. Most of the waterways were made navigable for both the intended residents and weekending families, and mooring fees and their rules and rates were strictly adhered to.

One sultry afternoon in the early 1970s, I conversed at Trent Lock with a self-confessed 'weekender boater' who was 'queuing', as he put it, to have his boat go through the lock and out onto the Trent. He was, I admit, the only boating person with whom I have spoken who was disgruntled. There were so many people using the waterways; many families with cars had become tired of queuing in traffic and others, like him, had taken to weekend boating along the network of waterways, only to find that they were queuing again at sets of lock gates. This was the substance of the man's complaint for as long as I stood beside him.

Meanwhile some local angling clubs bemoaned the fact that the occasional speedboat enthusiast was also using sections of the Erewash Canal and churning up the water surface at speeds estimated of around 35mph.

The 'pleasure boaters' of modern times, the British Waterways Board and the Environmental Agencies have done much to preserve our canals and have done all they can to maintain the traditions and lifestyles established by the canal pioneers. They should be recognised for their hard work and enthusiasm. Their work is their passion and in keeping waterways like the Erewash Canal open and running they benefit not just themselves but all interested parties, whether they are on land or water.

CHAPTER SIX

ALONG THE EREWASH CANAL

TRENT LOCK TO LONG EATON

At Trent Lock boaters are usually asked to keep the lock full with the top gates open, the exception being when the lock is in constant use. This happens during the busy half days of the main summer boating season. Facing the lock on the opposite side are the trees screening the natural wall of red stone and the cooling towers of the Ratcliffe-on-Soar Power Station.

This station and site was commissioned in 1967. With the lower buildings screened in places by pine plantations, which can be seen if one is leaving the M1 to take the Nottingham South exit, the entire site covers around 384 acres. Recognised as one of the largest and most effective power stations in the country, the cost of construction was in the region of £8.5 million.

An estimated twenty thousand tons of coal were, and perhaps still are, burnt every twenty-four hours. The Babcock and Wilcox boilers are capable of producing an astounding two tons of steam per second. The total energy output supplies the four MW turbine generators. Electricity, the end product, is then fed into the super grid of the Trent Valley at a rating of around 400,000 volts. Today the power station is fitted with a Flu Gas Desulphurisation Unit. This involves limestone interacting with gases; along with a gypsum producing process this eliminates a high percentage of sulphur dioxide.

Continuing by the lock and The Navigation Inn the regular walker realises that many changes have taken place. These changes have been imperceptible over short periods of time, but when photographs of the past are compared with those of the present the difference is very clear. Various hoists, cranes and jibs have been installed, used and removed, just as the boats moored on the opposite bank by the willow trees have changed in size and style. Across the field to the right is a private water, Fletchers Pond, used by an angling club. Nearby are a group of hedgeside chalets. These are private residences and should be regarded as such. The accommodation bridge is now gated on the Mills Dockyard side. Ahead, after the railway bridge, a bridge takes the towpath walker over an interesting mooring basin well concealed from the comparatively new bypass of Fields Farm Road.

This was called Sheet Stores Basin but more recently it has become known as Wyvern Marina, where both overnight and long-term moorings merge alongside boat building workshops, a crane and slipway, DIY repair shop and a licensed club. I was once told that coal was off-loaded from the boats here and reloaded onto the trains. It was also here that the tarpaulin sheets which were needed to cover railway wagons were manufactured and repaired, hence the basin's long-established name. A pronounced S-bend takes the waterway to the next bridge.

Moored boats with cooling towers in the background.

There are houses and gardens on both sides, but if I was writing in the 1950s I would be stressing the fact that the several fields of wheat or barley brought a particularly strong atmosphere of light and agriculture to the waterside scene over on the right.

The now landscaped garden which lies next to the buttresses of the Tamworth Road bridge reminds me of the account of the woman who lived there in the 1940s and '50s. Her quiet reminiscences about the swan pair that some years used to nest beneath the garden apple trees have stayed with me. Their existence is the reason why she and her husband left the lawn immediately around it unmown, to provide nesting material for the season ahead. This swan pair also nested on the bank of what is now Mills Dockyard and hatched off a brood of five or six cygnets. A year on they adopted a rear garden that had been allowed to go back to nature. Moorhens were constantly to be seen stilting between the towpath hedge and the fields of wheat or barley where, being land birds as well as water birds, they found an assortment of seeds and food particles.

The breeding swan pair in the 1930s and '40s apparently did not nest along the canal but in the reeds of nearby Barkers Pond, from where they padded with their cygnets behind them across the field to the canal when the cygnets were about six weeks old.

Traffic has also been held up along the B6540. After the bridge runs parallel with the canal a territorial swan pair have driven interloping swans off the canal and across the pavement. On the opposite side of the canal are school football and hockey pitches and the area's 'green lung', West Park. Extending for some 137 acres, West Park provides facilities and pitches for football, cricket, bowls, hockey and tennis. Beyond West Park and adjacent to the aptly named Wilsthorpe Road

Swans nesting beside Tamworth Road. Reeds allowed to take natural hold along our waterways provide nesting material for swans and moorhens.

is Trent College, surrounded by forty acres of gardens and playing fields. Trent College has long dominated the fields of engineering skills training and chemical tuition; its physics and biological laboratories are well to the fore.

During the 1990s a swan pair hatched off eight or nine cygnets along the roadside stretch. Having nested in the reeds that were allowed to grow out from the West Park bank on the opposite side. At the next bend, with Long Eaton Lock in sight, a bridge connects the facilities of West Park with the main shopping centre of Long Eaton. The adjacent street also takes the walker to the Library and Information Centre, a light, airy and much modernised facility, now regularly adorned with paintings by local artists.

The first aqueduct along the Erewash Canal takes the Golden Brook beneath it to meet the Trent. Surprisingly, the town of Long Eaton was a Welsh settlement until AD874. Local historians believe the settlement or town to have been called Wilsthorpe at this time, a name still commemorated by the road connecting the Derby Road to Sawley. When the Domesday Book was being compiled, the Anglo-Saxons named the settlement Aitone, which meant 'town beside the water'. Here one gains the impression that they used the trackways in the vicinity of New Tythe Street to reach the nearest point of the Trent, probably then in the region of Cranfleet Lock. Long Eaton Lock is where, like many a bygone boatman, I used to eat my lunchtime sandwiches when I was employed by Jay's the Furnishers, once situated on the corner of Regent Street.

Across the canal between the lock and the Derby Road Bridge stand the tenement mills which, at the beginning of the nineteenth century, employed half the working force of this

Long Eaton Mill beside the
Derby Road Bridge.

industrial town. The four-storey mills were designed with the intention of providing rentable space for several separate firms. The buildings attracted many businessmen, some with minimal capital, but they all signed agreements which ensured that the cost of power, electricity and business rates and the like was shared. The mills are typical of those built for the lace industry and were designed with many cast-iron window frames so as to provide adequate lighting for the employees. Turreted staircases of brick were also included. These provided the floor space that was required to cope with the hustle, bustle and generally productive activities that took place on either side of the long machines.

The buildings standing alongside the canal as one approaches Derby Road Bridge are called Bridge Mills and were completed in 1902. Where silver birches, willows and reeds gather just by the bridge buttresses, coal was offloaded with regularity. The other mills are West End Mill (1882) and Whiteley's Mill (1883). In the streets adjacent to these mills, across from the canal, are the Stanhope Mills – they are single storey – and the Harrington Mills (1885). The latest additions were the hard-walled Alexandra, Edward and Victoria Mills which were built in 1905/06.

The bridge crossing the canal at this point is not believed to be the original, while the road, known to everyone in the area as Derby Road, is now officially the A6005.

Passing beneath this relatively wide bridge, one cannot help but notice the mill and factory wall on the left, an area fringed by reeds. Further along where the feral mallard and moorhens choose to preen is a build-up of silt and reed partially screened by willows and alders. In the past, the 1920s and '40s perhaps, whichever swan pair chose this canal stretch for a breeding territory nested close to the wall where they could not be disturbed. To make a nest there birds pile reeds and aquatic vegetation high, in doing so they disarrange the seeds and shoots of the water plants around the nest.

Gradually new stands of reed and sprigs of waterside trees like willow and alder take hold within the silt and then regenerate to the benefit of other water life forms, birds and insects especially. The seeds and spores of various water plants are brought to the waterways on the feet and belly feathers of mallards, moorhens and swans, as well as on the hulls of boats.

At this point the towpath bypasses houses and gardens to the right and the factories and small engineering works of Bennett Street in Long Eaton to the left. Where the houses on the right end and the tracts of broken but well-conserved land begin, several once derelict fields divided by the River Erewash have been skilfully transformed and are now just a walk or bike ride away from a splendidly maintained nature reserve. Now known as Toton Washlands, the reserve consists of streams, pools and cutaways from the River Erewash, intertwining and planted with stands of reed, sedge, phrogmites and other kinds of plants beneficial to local wildlife. Thickets of haw, blackthorn and varying wild cherry types, the now maturing stands of teasel provide harvests for wintering birds – like the fieldfares and redwings – and bird flocks passing through.

All the finch species and titmice benefit, as well as the summering butterflies and daytime flying moths. Chiffs, chaff and willow warblers frequent the thickets throughout the breeding season along with other visiting warblers. Swallows and house martins 'hawk' for insects over the water surface. Early morning dog walkers flush snipe and redshank from the ponds and in late summer the expected dragonfly species are around in good number. In the 1960s this land tract was grazed by winter store cattle and a black horse with a white blaze. Local mothers who took their children in pushchairs to feed the horse sugar lumps were soon nicknaming it 'Nippy', and with good reason!

As for the canal, it levels off for a few hundred yards before reaching Dockholme Lock with the houses of Bennett Street over on the left. These properties were probably built in the 1920s and '30s. Some residents, maybe those with children, have fixed an ornamental barrier or two between the canal and the garden end. Others have allowed their lawns to grow down to the water's edge. Here and there a small boat or dinghy may be moored beside overhanging willows.

Herons, attracted to the several arms of swiftly flowing water dividing Toton Washlands, perch and preen in the garden willows and on the rooftops. Their singular and strangely nasal calls can be clearly heard in the night and still disturb the sleep of at least two local residents, so I'm told.

Dockholme Lock stands adjacent to a hump-backed bridge. This connects Bennett Street and the intertwining roads of Long Eaton and Sandiacre to the marshalling yards at Toton. The surfaced path and bridge crossing the River Erewash was once heavily used by shift workers employed at the railway sidings and marshalling yards, the buildings of which fringe the edge of Toton Washlands. These were once among the largest railway marshalling yards in Europe, and although it has experienced a marked decline over the past two or three decades it is now regarded as one of the largest diesel maintenance depots in the country. This next bend of the canal is typical in that houses, some with willow screened gardens, continue along the opposite side of the canal. At the same time store cattle graze rough pasture, and can be seen over the hedge on the right. There are two outflows or overflows, presumably cut and built to take surplus water down into the River Erewash, whose course can be plotted by following with the eye the line of willows and alders which rise well in front of the marshalling yards.

These houses were built in the 1950s. Where the canal turns noticeably north, allotments replace the houses. The hedgerow and surrounding land tracts still hold a thriving population of that fast declining bird, the house sparrow. In this area, probably because the farm buildings and land nurture many seed grasses and stands of thickets, these intriguing birds are around in good number.

The next bridge and lock are particularly well known, for as the towpath rises to meet with the lock gates the well-preserved Sandiacre Lock Cottage adds a further vein of intrigue to the waterside scene. Long the meeting place of the Erewash Canal Preservation and Development Association, these picturesque lock cottages are regarded as a local showpiece by boaters and towpath ramblers and are mentioned by almost everyone who has explored the Erewash Canal. Beyond the cottage an arm of the canal swings left to the bridge beside the farm. In the past narrowboat men travelling the Derby Canal paid their tolls here, for this waterway began its journey at the now defunct lock gates beyond here. Originally narrowboat men were required to pay their tolls for the Derby Canal at the Sandiacre–Erewash lock house at least until the Derby Canal Company established a toll house on the opposite side.

The bridge at Sandiacre Lock was much used by boatmen and farm workers and to my mind the nearby farm buildings are part of the 'showpiece scene', whether they are intended to be or not. Forty or fifty years ago a dairy herd would cross this hump-backed bridge twice daily on its journey to and from the milking sheds. Go back another sixty or seventy years and one can imagine farm workers, lock-keepers and narrowboat people meeting to exchange pleasantries and have a smoke while ducks and geese padded around their feet. One or two elderly folk here recall the farm being owned by the Fletcher brothers, George and Billy, and later by Bowley's, the Sandiacre butchers. Across the field glimpses of water enhance the hedgerow scene, for here is a lake known as the Ballast Hole. This was again a railway pond from which ballast had been dug to raise and make the railway embankment. Like most ponds of this type, it is managed by an angling club and probably has been for some years.

The Ballast Hole is best seen from the seat of a Red Arrow Express coach when one is travelling between Nottingham and Derby. In the winter months, when the surrounding trees are bereft of foliage, this tract of water appears sizeable and oval in shape. It is one of the few ponds in the area to which, I'm assured, there is no public right of way.

The great embankment and bridge supports of the A52 Nottingham–Derby road always remind me of how far we have come with regard to modern construction engineering – all the more so when I am beneath the bridge and tolerating the consistent roar of traffic.

To a visitor exploring only the towpath of the Erewash Canal, I should point out that these fourteen or so miles of the A52 linking Nottingham with Derby are now officially known as the Brian Clough Way, in honour of the legendary late football manager who lived at nearby Stapleford.

In one of the houses on the opposite side of the canal I conversed in the 1960s with a lady who had lived there for many years; in quieter times I frequently saw one or more kingfishers perched on the front garden gate. The next stage along this waterway, which runs in parallel with the busy Longmoor Lane and its continuous files of traffic, is the bridge that crosses the original Nottingham–Derby turnpike road at Sandiacre.

Accommodation bridge still used daily by cowmen at Sandiacre Lock.

Modern-day leisure routed signpost, Sandiacre Lock.

Derby Road Bridge, Sandiacre. (Courtesy of ECPDA)

SANDIACRE TO STANTON GATE

Conversing recently with eighty-six-year-old Leslie Severn, I learned that the bridge beneath which we pass today is the second bridge to have spanned the canal here. When one takes the turnpike road into consideration perhaps it is even the third. Leslie remembers the Old Coal Wharf on the right which stood opposite Padmore Moorings. In his boyhood, workmen were to be seen spading coal off the moored boats into wheelbarrows, which they then wheeled into the yard adjacent to the towpath. They then spaded the coal from the wheelbarrows out onto the carts, each was braked but would have been ready to be pulled to the assorted depots and businesses by a horse. Quite a large proportion of the coal would have been bagged, probably in that same yard.

When one considers the human energy that was expended in operations such as this, is it any wonder that the people of the past had shorter lifespans than we do today, as medical advances ease us into the high-tech, microchip world of the twenty-first century?

Across the canal is Padmore Moorings, a cluster of small shops, a post office and the Red Lion Hotel. Not surprisingly, this corner, with the lights controlling the offset crossroads alongside the hump-backed canal bridge, is known locally as Red Lion Square. Padmore Moorings are named to commemorate Mr G.R. Padmore, who was employed as a clerk for the Sandiacre Parish Council. A row of ornamental cherry trees, lawns and plots for seasonal flowers enhance the moorings. Alongside is an information plaque informing the towpath explorer that a lime kiln was situated beside the Old Coal Wharf. Here lime was produced for spreading on the fields. It was also sold to the brickworks situated close to the Derby Canal on Bostock's Lane.

Derby Road Bridge, Sandiacre, in 2006.

Angling Club notice panel.

Padmore Moorings.

As the canal bends the chimney of the mill immediately catches the eye. The small modern industrial estate, built on the site of the now derelict lime works and coal wharf, also attracts the attention. This mill, Springfield Mill, was built relatively late (in 1888), specifically for the production of lace. The next footbridge spanning the waterway brings to mind the recollections of a friend who was employed on the railways. One winter morning he crossed the bridge at the same time as a barn owl chose to perch on a fence rung close to the River Erewash. The owl seemed to have located prey. It allowed my friend close enough to see the cigarette ash coloured spots standing out against its other yellow-brown wing plumage before it took wing. Tracts of derelict land, interweaving between railways and canals, serve as breeding grounds for countless rodents and small birds. Consequently, barn owls patrol such areas, usually by night, and sparrowhawks by day.

On the flatter, wet fields closer to Stanton Gate, at least one pair of kestrels can be seen hovering against the background of two wooded escarpments: Stapleford Wood and the old Bramcote Manor Wood respectively. When the fields meet with the sandy bays of the canal over on the left the higher levels of Sandiacre dominate the horizon. The church built on the ridge known as 'Stoney Clouds' may have existed before Norman times, but it was not overlooked by these great church builders. Work known to be of Norman design enhances part of the interior as well as the carvings. The front is also known to have been built around 600 years ago.

The low-lying fields are grazed by horses and ponies and there appears to be a riding school up on the ridge by the locally famed 'Stoney Clouds'. The fields in the summer are yellow with buttercups, celandines and other wild flowers. To the right, as the northbound railway closes in, a series of small and reeded railway ponds attract the local folk, many of whom are looking for frog and newt spawn in the early spring. Unfortunately more mallard and moorhen eggs are taken than is generally realised.

Padmore Moorings and Springfield Mill.

Pastures Lock with church and 'Stoney Clouds' in the background.

The aptly named Pastures Lock is aided by an outflow and is a popular place for present-day boaters needing a snack before continuing their journey. The next bridge with reeds screening the buttress is on the Sandiacre side. What appears to be a modernised farm cottage or holding overlooking the water is alongside. Its presence speaks of the fact that a once lucrative industry is now long gone. It is known as Stanton Gate.

STANTON GATE TO GALLOWS INN

From the Ilkeston side of the Stanton Gate bridge one can see – on either side of the canal – tracts of land that, serve as nature reserves, as well as pony grazing; in some cases these reserves are unattended. Beyond the M1 bridge woods come down to the water's edge. All the summer warbler species can be heard singing here. By day moorhens are ferrying their young and searching for food through the reed fringes. At night they roost high in the hawthorn thickets.

The entire derelict field network from hereon is patterned by fox trails. Meadowsweet and teasel can hardly be missed. There are yellow water lilies and yellow flag irises in their seasons, while stands of water mint along with butterflies, peacocks, red admirals, tortoiseshell and common blues indicate that the food plants nurtured by these species are there in good number.

The Stanton Works railway bridge and Stanton Lock are interesting in that the Nutbrook Trail begins by crossing the bridge so that the Erewash Canal is on the right. This is obviously an old industrial way which leads to the fenced sheds and main buildings of Stanton Ironworks. Across from the canal a sculpture has been erected to commemorate the toil and industry of those who once worked here. The sculpture consists of a combination of chains and pipework, both products closely associated with this once-important site.

Meanwhile, along the canal towpath and beyond Hallam Fields Lock the sealed entrance to the now defunct Nutbrook Canal again reminds the canal explorer of the tons of pipework and supports that were transported through here en route for the Trent, the Soar and the Grand Union Canal system beyond. The little Nutbrook Canal extended for some 4½ miles into the Shipley and Heanor coal measure country. It bypassed the wharves of Stanton Ironworks – of which comparatively little can be seen today. The foremost canal section was demolished in 1962. Along this second stretch two successive outflows descend, and from a series of reedy sections it meanders into the silver birch and willow tract where the overflow water from the canal joins the River Erewash. There are stands of silver birch and varied poplars between the towpath and the sports fields which are interspersed by small industrial estates. The second aqueduct is here.

The locality on the left, intersected by the hilly winding crossroad of Quarry Hill, of which one need only be aware if one is a motorist, is called Hallam Fields. The residential area and extended village of West Hallam lies beyond.

GALLOWS INN TO COTMANHAY

The next bridge and lock are named after the pub alongside, The Gallows Inn. Believed to have been built around 1765, the pub was first called The Crown, but by 1798 the name had been changed to that by which we know it today, although for a brief period in the 1990s the name was altered to The Lock, Stock and Barrel. A year or two later it reverted to The Gallows Inn, the name by which most of the local population had known it throughout their lives.

Bearing this name, the pub serves as an historical reference pointer, there having once been a gallows close by. The gallows were built when the plague was raging in the City of Nottingham.

Passing through Pastures Lock.

Pastures Lock from the Stanton side.

The scene beyond Pastures Lock.

Narrowboats and loaders at Stanton Ironworks Wharf. (Courtesy of Mike Taylor, *The River Trent Navigation*, 2000)

A sculpture on The Nutbrook Trail.

The Gallows Inn, Ilkeston.

Criminals were tried and executed despite the plague, but why Ilkeston was chosen as an alternative site for the gallows is not known. It was, however, a site on which all those involved with the judicial system agreed. Therefore, those found guilty made the last journey of their lives, no doubt by cart, from Nottingham to within an estimated few yards of the pub site. The gallows remained until they blew down in a storm in 1870.

The pub which is currently to be found beside the towpath was built by local brewer Joseph Shipstone in 1936. It has been refurbished several times. In these types of pubs mulled ale would have been drunk by the boat people – probably on quite a regular basis. Ilkeston, the third largest town in Derbyshire, is situated way off up the hill to the left. A town dealing with marketing goods and textiles, several of the streets lead off from the sheltered and compact square where the weekend market is held. The nearby church of St Mary dates from 1150. In October a three-day fair, a cut-off from the Nottingham Goose Fair, is staged in the Market Place.

At the lock gates and across from the pub the steps – or stone foot grips – are well preserved. These were built to help whoever was pushing the lock gates and were intended to be supportive during times of hard frost, snow and slush. They may not, on reflection, be the original foot grips but rather replacements, although I know of no one who can verify this or say otherwise in as far as the dating of them is concerned.

Leaving The Gallows Inn, the canal bends and there are small industrial units positioned to the right of the towpath and houses with gardens on the left. In the early 1970s, and probably for many years before, a tangle of willow thickets had taken root where the houses and gardens stand today. As is typical of the locality, the thickets were referred to as 'T' Willow Woods' where, no doubt, many a local lad made his first den and birds nested with regularity.

A field, sports pitches and a pond separate the houses from a tract of allotments which are used in various ways. Then an interesting lock and hump-backed bridge comes into sight. This is Greens Lock; there is a wharf – or winding hole – on the higher pound beyond the lock gates. A narrow footpath leads off from the bridge and into the Ilkeston suburbs. This narrow route was obviously used by canal workers, as well as the lock-keeping families at Greens Lock and possibly the local colliers. Houses flank the waterway to the left and the railway levels with the towpath to the right. Beyond the railway the green slopes and fields of Cossall and the western edge of the D.H. Lawrence country sweep away all images of heavy industry. Here too, if one follows the hedge line along the field of land below the horizon, the winding course of the Nottingham Canal is discernible.

There is also a gated railway crossing the point where a tract leads up between the fields to the towpath of the Nottingham Canal and the delightfully rural village of Cossall, where the fiancée of D.H. Lawrence, Louise Burrows, once lived. Cossall rises well above the canal, with a main street twisting narrowly between residential gardens. In the churchyard there is a distinctive memorial to a villager who, serving as a soldier, was killed at Waterloo.

Because the Nottingham Canal was routed through relatively high ridge countryside, at least considering the land contours in the area, it has long been known as the 'Top Cut'. The Erewash Canal, gauged through the marshy tracts winding around the eastern peripheries of several Derbyshire towns, is known as 'Bottom Cut'.

On the left the fields, once bypassed by the narrowboat people – who transported their consignments of coal along the section of the Erewash Canal, have been developed to cope with the recreational needs of the housing estate residents. Consequently the rural atmosphere blends with that of recreation and invites wanderers like myself to linger for a while around Potters Lock. There is little to remind those using the canal and its towpath in modern times of the lock-keepers' cottages at Greens or Potters Lock. But the latter place would have been an idyllic spot in summers past, although it was undoubtedly at the mercy of the snowstorms and freezing conditions that characterised almost every 'canal age' winter.

The inn signs.

Well-preserved stone grips, The Gallows Inn.

Greens Lock, Ilkeston.

After Potters Lock and its narrowly spanning bridge, the course of the canal bends noticeably and rises above a marshy tract of the Erewash Valley down to the right. From Potters Lock the canal route extends to Black's Bridge, Ilkeston, with houses and grass banks coming down to the water on the opposite bank. Black's Bridge connects the busy Station Road to the uphill streets of Ilkeston with the new bypasses linking the pleasant nearby villages of Cossall and Awsworth. The River Erewash and its flood meadows have, in comparatively recent times, been channelled. The reed beds around Ilkeston Junction have been overlaid by surfaces of tarmacadam, upon which car showrooms and workshop businesses are now well established.

At the end of Green Lane, on an afternoon of freezing fog some thirty years ago, I recall hearing the repetitive quacking of Aylesbury ducks. This is a sound which the canal users must have heard frequently. In the winters it often erupted through the fogs which I remember as being thicker than those that we have known in recent years. Ducks and geese were kept on most waterways, for their eggs as well as their food value. One or two of the old terraced type houses had front doors which all but opened out onto the canal bank. This was where swans stood waiting for bread to be thrown. Rats were often a secondary consideration when householders were arriving at or leaving their properties.

Beyond Black's Bridge, where the canal bends yet again, there are 'flash' pools in the meadows which are divided by the River Erewash to the right. At this point a reedy tract appears which runs almost level with the two blocks of cottages and garages. The bridge ahead was not designed for the kind of traffic we know today. It is quite a difficult, bottleneck-type bridge, and traffic lights have been installed to lessen the possibility of accidents.

Potters Lock accommodation bridge.

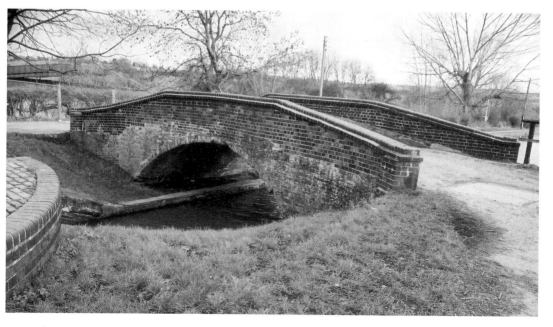

There are many accommodation bridges along the Erewash Canal.

Rural and recreational scenes merge beyond Potters Lock.

By the bridge on the opposite side is the aptly named Bridge Inn that was once regularly frequented by narrowboat people. To the right Newtons Lane bypasses the water meadows and meanderings of the River Erewash. The uphill sweep then leads up to the new bypass and the ridge, still holding the much-used but unnavigable course of the Nottingham Canal. On the opposite side of the Erewash Canal to The Bridge Inn stands a relatively newly built property called The Moorings. A timber yard used to stand on this site and the grandfather of a friend ran his timber merchant business from here. He would pay either the Erewash Canal Company or British Waterways a toll or rent that allowed him to drain overflow water from the canal into the timber yard to drive his mill wheels.

This is Barker's Lock and one can imagine there being a lock house on the site of the timber yard. The Moorings has only been added in recent times. There are more houses to the left with grass bank recreational strips, while to the right is a scrap yard for Volvo cars and a coal washing plant. The next lock is Stensons, but at the time of writing it remained unnamed. Coming in from the right and spanning the canals and River Erewash is the Bennerley Viaduct. This trestle structure was completed in 1877. A structure was needed that would be capable of crossing 500 yards of quite precarious ground, precarious in that there were water meadows beneath which were being used for coal extraction and ironstone tunnelling. The Midland Railway also passed over these meadows.

The shareholders of the Great Northern Railway decided upon a viaduct structure of wrought iron and a lattice and trestle type design, known as 'the warren' style. This design had been patented in 1848 and was known to be successful. As a serving viaduct the Bennerley withstood all threats of ground erosion until the line was closed in 1968. It is now a Grade II

The Bridge Inn and Barkers Lock, Ilkeston.

The Moorings, Barkers Lock, Ilkeston, on an iced-over February morning.

listed building. From here the canal accompanies the towpath in a relatively straight section to Cotmanhay.

The abrupt hump-backed bridge beside the second Bridge Inn along the route at Cotmanhay has been graffiti splashed in recent times, which is why I chose to photograph the pub and its sign rather than the bridge. In the welcoming lounge I was surprised to see more framed photographs of railways and trams than of the canal and its narrowboat people. When my companion Denis Astle asked if there was a reason for this, we both learned that indeed there was: although at first glance a waterman's pub, The Bridge Inn was apparently used regularly by the railwaymen. The trams from the centre of Ilkeston and other parts terminated at the canal bridge within six strides of the windows. Thus one is left with the impression of a very busy little hostelry, doing business at a time when mulled ale was served with regularity and ice-cream sellers collected ice chunks from the near solidified water surface of the canal as a means of refrigeration.

The silver birch tract which served to front the Bennerley Viaduct and screen the railway has, in recent months, been given the name Bennerley Woodlands. Directly opposite the hump-backed bridge is one of the several paths in the area that cut alongside the pony paddocks and scrubland to connect with the towpath of the Nottingham Canal. Continuing north along the towpath, as the railway closes in again on the long bend, the small pond at the foot of the recently strengthened embankment is high with the long stemmed plant that I believe is phragmite. Small birds like reed buntings and wagtails frequent such areas, as do daytime-flying moths, moorhens and possibly even the secretive water rail.

One retired railwayman told me that he had cycled along the towpath from Cotmanhay to Langley Mill every working day for twenty-nine years and each April a swan pair built a nest between the railway embankment and towpath and hatched off a brood. The railway to the right crosses the canal and in days gone by the trains presumably pulled in at Shipley Station. A relatively short, straight length of the canal takes the boaters, towpath walker or cyclist to the interesting Shipley Gate Bridge and the pleasantly sited Shipley Lock.

The Shipley Gate Lane crosses the canal here. On the canal's immediate left is a stableyard still used by equestrians. A walk up the lane a few yards – towards the footbridge over the railway – takes you to the sturdy white building which is now an entertainment centre but was once The Shipley Boat Inn. Exactly when this hostelry was built is not entirely clear, but it was not called The Shipley Boat Inn without good reason. The boatyard people had only to walk a hundred yards to reach this popular venue, and in the 1970s and '80s when it was a pub/restaurant with disco facilities many of them did!

On my first summer evening exploration of Shipley Lock I was surprised to see streams of young girls strolling elegantly across the bridge in various intriguing forms of dress. They were all intent on a drinking and disco session at The Shipley Boat Inn. Leaning on the lock, I mused on how the heads of those old narrowboat men would have turned had they been moored there with a catwalk of young models walking passed them.

I was once told that there were two venues on the lane called The Shipley Boat Inn. However, when I asked the young woman bolting and chaining the gate of the stableyard about this, she seemed surprised and claimed to know of 'only the one' – the original. However, she did point out the mill beyond the houses and gardens on the Eastwood side of the canal and the cottage with the lovely garden situated alongside Shipley Lock. This used to be, she explained, The Old Slaughterhouse. A plaque on the gate verified this.

Pit ponies, and perhaps the occasional towpath horse, were put down here when they were badly injured or in poor condition. An official slaughter man was on hand to do the job, but whether he lived on the site or not is not known. Nor can anyone say for certain whether or

The bridge in question.

The Bridge Inn sign, Cotmanhay.

The Bannerley Viaduct, now a Grade II listed structure.

Shipley Lock sheened with thin ice.

The Old Slaughterhouse beside Shipley Lock.

not the private residence was a lock-keeper's cottage before it was used as a slaughterhouse. The last of the slaughter men, I am told, was Robert Moon. The slaughterhouse closed in 1962.

I become so carried away by the tranquillity here that it is difficult to imagine it as so busy a place that boats and consignments had to be regulated. Its importance to trade would have escaped me had I overlooked a slim but informative volume, *The Erewash Canal*, which was produced by members of the Erewash Canal Preservation and Development Association. I found this on the reference shelves in the Long Eaton Library and Information Centre and discovered that the boats and consignments were overseen or regulated according to how many there were to a canal pound. The narrowboat people were told where they should be moored and when they could leave. The overall scene would have been one of colour and progression, with consignments of baled cotton coming down from Cromford Wharf which would have been sheeted by tarpaulin alongside consignments of coal and occasionally oil.

Today it is difficult to imagine this tranquil spot as coal seam country. However, just over the bridge at Shipley Lock – opposite the towpath – was Dukes Wharf, the industrial line of transportable coal. At one time Dukes Wharf was believed to have been among those listed as holding the busiest wharf-orientated workforce in Great Britain. It was not unusual for consignments of coal to be transported from Shipley to London, via the lower route this book is exploring.

The coal seam hills of Mapperley and Shipley were to the west and a wooden tramway was soon opened to link the areas. The local historians tell me, it ran parallel with the lane that passes over the canal today. The tramway extended for two or three miles into the heart of the colliery

Confirmatory sign, although this is now a private residence.

The Aqueduct at Shipley. I learned from an ECPDA publication that this aqueduct was made on dry land.

regions, those working on it – when time and energy allowed – would have had a few tales to tell about its operation! However, in 1795 the collieries switched to the Nutbrook Canal, which had been built for the express purpose of transporting coal. The boats and barges continued along the four or so miles to the now unrecognisable Junction Lock, just south of Ilkeston. It was at this point that the journey down the Erewash Canal, across the Trent and up the Soar, began.

Dukes Wharf became less busy around 1847–48 when the Erewash Valley Railway was opened. A branch line or two connecting the Miller-Mundy owned collieries led to a notable decline in consignments from the Shipley coal fields. However, when the Nutbrook Canal began to suffer leakages and problems with its water levels business soon reverted to Dukes Wharf. By 1895 prosperity had returned and a third rail link was established following the closure of the Nutbrook Canal.

A rail siding, triangular in shape, was built so that one side would stay parallel to the wharf which would hopefully ease unloading. At least, this was the intention of the collective management grouping, although their direct experience of 'unloading' was probably minimal to say the least. It was at this time that restraints were placed on the canal boats, to avoid bottleneck-type problems those boat people wishing to enter the wharf for loading had little choice but to moor some 140–150 yards downstream of the lock. There were regular instances of double-mooring while agreements were also reached with the Nottingham and Cromford Canal companies for extra water to be daily supplied to the lock chambers.

Dukes Wharf was apparently still operational at this time but business was declining. By the early years of the Second World War this decline was apparent to all and its earlier status as a hub was becoming a distant memory. For me my favourite time to be here is in the quiet of

Looking back towards Shipley Lane and the horizon woods.

a winter afternoon, for this is the most rural stretch of Erewash Canal's 11¾-mile route. Over towards Shipley the fields slope and woods with interesting tree traceries are outlined against the sky. This idyllic scene is often enhanced by the clouds or low sunlight. Stoats and weasels are occasionally to be seen hunting the towpath hedgerows and a kestrel is often hovering above the fields. If I drove the narrow Shipley Gate Lane at night, I would expect to see the occasional barn owl similarly quartering the hedgerows, especially with a ruined mill and stableyards in close proximity.

A mere 200–300-yard walk from the picturesque Shipley Lock and one finds that the River Erewash diverts beneath it. Here there is a particularly well-known viaduct, where the river swings in from the Shipley side and turns, before turning again towards Eastwood. Birdwatchers should quietly linger here, as the low branches of alder and willow are those used by kingfishers which perch close to the water surface in order to locate the small fish on which they feed. Pied and grey wagtails, the insect feeders, frequent the same type of habitat.

Eastwood Lock is where, for the first time, the towpath crosses from right to left. I am told that the towpath is always on the shallower side of the waterway. On the hill to the east is the old mining town of Eastwood. D.H. Lawrence, the famous novelist, poet and artist, was born at 8A Victoria Street in the town. An early section of his novel *Sons and Lovers* was set in Eastwood. Literary interpretative guides can tell those interested more about his life there.

Round the bend from Eastwood Lock there are pleasant views across the fields to the left. Soon the hedgerow takes over and a bridge connects what appears to be a farm with the Eastwood road/bypass on the higher ground to the east. The canal bank here has receded on the edge of the field and consequently stands of reed, sedge and phragmites have taken hold, thus providing habitat for several interesting species of wildlife. Beyond this point the canal proceeds in a pronounced S-bend; interesting woody hedgerows line the route while the fields in the background vale are the last along the route.

Eventually another lane bridge crosses the canal. To the left is a solid looking house that in the past may have served as both a farm and a pub. On the right is a chalet park with well-tended gardens. There is a strong, and really rather enviable feeling of isolation and self-sufficiency about the site. Even so, there is still a strong sense of attachment between the canal and its traffic, particularly on Sundays when there is a rally at the Great Northern Basin. It is then that the boats cleave the water; they are splendidly coloured and often continue in file as they make for the last bridge.

Boats from Gainsborough, Brayford Pool, Lincoln, Stoke-on-Trent, Barton-under-Needwood and other intriguing waterway locations make their way to Nottinghamshire on these occasions. Old friendships are re-established and new ones are made, while the bond felt between those with a passion for the waterways ensures a great atmosphere, regardless of the season or weather.

A factory site then flanks the towpath to the left. Brambles provide shelter for the ubiquitous moorhens, who in the summer become rivals, hold breeding territories, but sometimes form flocks of between twenty and thirty, on the right. At the Great Northern Basin bridge a plaque welcomes boaters to the site. This plaque was erected by the Erewash Canal Preservation and Development Association, the members of which are always genial hosts, beyond the lock gates.

CHAPTER SEVEN

LANGLEY MILL – GREAT NORTHERN BASIN

In 1794 the Cromford, Nottingham and Erewash canals were linked at Langley Bridge. The Erewash Canal terminated on the opposite side of the Great Northern Basin. A factory car park has since been built on the site. I first saw this termination point when I cycled the route in the late 1950s. At the time there was little of significance to see, except a reed bed on the left side of the bridge. The reeds had probably grown in what was once a loading bay or wharf.

The Great Northern Basin was planned and overseen by the great engineer William Jessop, thus the Cromford and Erewash canals became a merging through-route extending for some twenty-six miles. The original name was probably the Langley Bridge or Langley Mill Basin, and this name would have remained until the Great Northern Railway Company purchased the entire complex.

This was also the tramway terminus for routes leading west or eastward out of, or into, Langley Mill. One tramline, opened in 1797, connected the basin tollhouse and the Great Northern Inn to the Brinsley Colliery. The termination point of the Nottingham Canal is significant in modern times in that it is situated at the renovated swing bridge beside the Great Northern Inn.

Ike Argent, on learning of my boyhood towpath explorations along the Nottingham Canal to the Wollaton Colliery, pointed out the lock gates. He went on to explain that the top gates (those closest to the basin) were, under his guidance, removed from the Wollaton Colliery pound known as 'Warm Waters' when that length of the canal was closed in the 1960s. The gates closest to the bridge buttresses, the bottom gates, are the originals, although changes are scheduled, possibly soon after this book has gone into print.

The towpath is foreshortened today, as is the land tract to the right; this is due to the area beyond having been designated as private moorings. There is, understandably, no car parking space for visitors. Those who stroll the short paths must show respect both for the natural environment and their fellow visitors. The vast majority of people do act in the way expected of them, and that is good to see.

To the left of the towpath, partially surrounded by trees, is the pump house. This was built from brick and was designed to take up very little room. The pumps were to be used in times of need to take the water from the lower canal stretch round to the upper. An earlier publication gave me the impression that the water was pumped directly from the nearby River Erewash, and indeed it may have served this purpose originally. The truth is that no one today can say for sure.

Nearby is a timber store where planks of considerable length, known as stopping planks, are stored in readiness to dam sections of the waterway should repair work need to be undertaken.

The Nottingham Canal arm of the Great Northern Basin.

The splendid pub sign.

This occasionally happens and, as stated earlier, it has the effect of shortening the towpath. A Severn Trent notice by the pump house explains that the cleaned water – which has been returned from the eight sewage plants – makes up more than the river's flow in itself. More plans for recycled, clean water are also given, along with Severn Trent's promise to spend £44 million to improve the water facilities of the future.

On the last February morning I spent on the towpath with Denis Astle I was introduced to Peter Brookes, a friend of Denis's from his schooldays. Peter, now retired from the railways, has a narrowboat built with a splendidly economical interior which speaks of self-sufficiency and asks the question: 'Who could ask for more?' Surrounded by books on transport history and maps of waterway routes, we sipped tea while discussing the various sets of locks and accommodation bridges along the route. Not surprisingly, the friendship and expertise of Ike Argeant cropped up; along with his own waterway journals Peter has – with a friend – penned *The Ballad of Ike Argeant*, which may yet interest a publisher.

As the compiler of this book, I am aware of a shortfall in the names and social histories of the families who worked or lived beside the Langley Mill or Great Northern, at least when compared with those at Trent Lock who I have described. At this meeting point of the Erewash, Cromford and Nottingham canals there were navvies, lock-keepers, narrowboat families, boat builders, maintenance teams and others with occupations linked to the waterways, but of whom little is known. That said, they were obviously resilient people whose lifestyles – like those of all watermen and transporting people – were considerably harder than we can appreciate today.

Into the moorings at the Great Northern Basin.

Peter Brookes, canal enthusiast and co–author of *The Ballad of Ike Argeant*.

The Pump House, Great Northern Basin.

It is difficult to establish exactly when The Great Northern pub was built. It has been described as a seventeenth-century pub, but in recent times I have been assured that it was here, or that there was at least a pub on the site, in the sixteenth century. Who can say how many names it has been given over the centuries? It may have been standing when John Varley and the Pinkerton brothers surveyed the route of their intended canal. In their day it could well have been a coaching inn. At some time in its relatively long life the pub was probably called The Bridge, in common with most pubs sited beside a bridge and lock throughout the British Isles.

The Great Northern was the name given to the pub when the railway company bought the property and the canal basin. It is thought that the purchase happened some time in the mid-eighteenth century. Today it is a popular resort; catering for families it provides welcoming bars, a carvery and a games room, all of which were established beneath those old, low beams. Nor will the railway and tram enthusiast be disappointed, as there are far more framed photographs, prints and drawings of steam trains and trams than there are of boats. It was, after all, a railwayman's pub as much as a narrowboat man's.

On the black-painted beams in one bar the colloquial sayings, phrases and mannerisms of speech are painted in white lettering. The most prominent, which can still be heard from here and into the cities of Nottingham and Derby, is, 'Looks black over Bill's Motthaz',[*] which a reference alongside translates for the layman: 'It might rain shortly.' Another is 'Gizzadrag',[*] which we learn is to be interpreted as, 'Can I have a puff of your cigarette?', while one that must have been used by colliers, canal maintenance and railway workers for generations is, 'Giyit sum welly youth!'[*] roughly translated as, 'Hit it as hard as you can old bean!' These quirks, which give some indication of the sense of identity felt by locals, adds greatly to the charm of The Great Northern, which should be visited by everyone exploring the basin and canal.

THE RESTORATION PROJECT

Aided by excerpts from local newspaper cuttings I once attempted to follow the restoration programme. Sadly I failed to take part because I lacked a car and was working on some of the weekends scheduled for the main tasks.

In the 1970s the Erewash Canal Preservation and Development Association approached the Nottinghamshire and Derbyshire Councils to try and get the canal recognised as a leisure amenity. Both councils, after weeks of pressure, agreed to grant joint financial aid to the venture. Delighted members of the association decided that the lock leading into the Langley Mill Basin should be restored and the entire basin dredged, their reasoning being that when these tasks were completed boats could be moored and turned round accordingly.

In 1972 the now well-established magazine *Waterways World* stated in its inaugural issue that the *Mai-Arde* was the first boat to enter the lock. However, according to my informant, that item of reportage was somewhat premature, due to the lock being without paddle gear and gates. In a relatively short time boats began using the lock; they moored and turned much as the society members had originally envisaged.

---

[*]These phrases were originally taken from Scollins, Richard and Titford, John, *Ey Up Mi Duck! Dialect of Derbyshire and the East Midlands* (Countryside Books, 2000)

THE PUMP HOUSE

OWNED & RESTORED BY
E.C.P.D.A.
WITH SUPPORT FROM I.W.A.W.R.G.
& MANY VOLUNTEERS
TO PROVIDE BACK PUMPING
FOR THE G.N. BASIN &
CROMFORD CANAL

Confirmation of back pumping here.

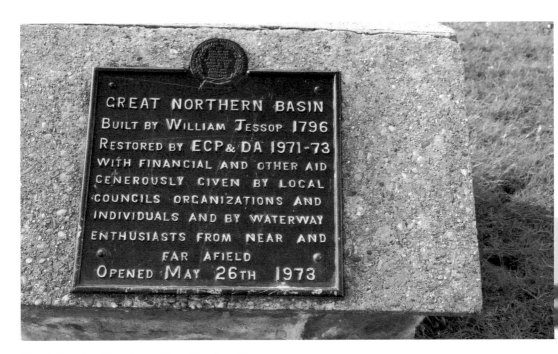

GREAT NORTHERN BASIN
BUILT BY WILLIAM JESSOP 1796
RESTORED BY ECP & DA 1971-73
WITH FINANCIAL AND OTHER AID
GENEROUSLY GIVEN BY LOCAL
COUNCILS ORGANIZATIONS AND
INDIVIDUALS AND BY WATERWAY
ENTHUSIASTS FROM NEAR AND
FAR AFIELD
OPENED MAY 26TH 1973

Grand Opening Day plaque, Great Northern Basin.

How many miles from…?

The Erewash Canal termination point at Langley Mill in 1962.

The cost of providing adequate mooring facilities was estimated that year as £1,800. This money would enable the all-important excavating plant to be fully functional when it was required. Working parties were continually being set up and volunteers gave their time freely to restore the basin. Some groups worked on Friday afternoons while others would continue into the weekends.

The project was run efficiently: the professional help and advice that had been sought ensured that things ran smoothly while council officials kept the financial support constant. The excavations and general repair works were well planned, publicity for the project came by way of the local newspapers and at least one – brief – early evening television slot. Much was achieved during the winter of 1972/73, much of which was thanks to the goodwill of local companies, for example an Ilkeston haulage company who loaned out their lorries throughout most, if not all, of the restoration project.

Consequently silt, spoil, rubble and dumped domestic rubbish was removed by the stalwart society workers and supporters. They believed, and have since been vindicated, that the basin could be restored and managed as moorings with a maintenance site and much else besides. The swing bridge was reactivated and a wall was constructed. The real sense of achievement created a real bond within the association; the strength of the ties were established is still apparent some thirty-odd years later. Sixty to seventy boats were assembled for the opening rally which was attended, I am told, by 'something like 4,000 people'.

The official opening, on 26 May 1973, proved to be the crowning glory of a restoration project that attracted many plaudits at the time and is viewed in an increasingly positive manner as the years pass. Its success has been mainly due to the interest and enthusiasm of all the association members, both past and present. Their sights are now set on helping with the restoration of the Derby Canal which, like the Erewash, has a stalwart band of supporters. May they go from strength to strength.

CHAPTER EIGHT

DOWNSTREAM OF TRENT LOCK

Boats and boaters travelling downstream are reminded by the guides and signs, if they are Nottinghamshire bound, to bear left at the Nottingham Sailing Clubhouse and enter the Cranfleet Cut. Far more boats line the banks here today than did in the 1950s and '60s. The railway bridge and line was the one targeted by German bombers in the Second World War. Quite a number of the moored boats are owned by members of the Nottingham Sailing Club, which is basically a yacht enthusiast's resort. It is home to some unconventional crafts: one of these moored boats, I was told, had been completely made from wood. But, I asked myself, surely the hull was of steel?

That intriguing atmosphere of waterside self-sufficiency is also to be found here. Bicycles are roped into hedgerows, piles of kindling lie on the grass, large tree branches need sawing and waterproofs are spread out on the hedge. A woman boater told of how, in recent years, she had watched an otter while taking out a rowing boat and had explored the Thrumpton shallows below the weir. She also delighted in having a kingfisher perch on her line post most bright mornings.

A young man from Essex, pegging down and roping his boat during a severe February gale, told me that despite the rigorous exercise and discipline that characterised life on the water he would never live anywhere but on a canal boat. All the boaters with whom I have spoken are dedicated to their chosen way of life.

One man had lived on the Cranfleet Cut since the early 1970s. He echoed the widespread sentiment that he would not live in anything but a canal boat. He smiled as he mused on the fact that if he chose a more modern form of transport he could travel to his northern home town in two and a half hours. By boat the journey would take two and a half weeks. Still, of course he would rather travel by boat.

There is a splendid white accommodation bridge spanning the Cranfleet, beyond which sheep graze the flat fields of what I believe are the Thrumpton Hall estate. The Trent and its descending weir coil out of view below the wooded banks on the far side. Towpath explorers, like myself, walk the Cranfleet banks. Families ramble leisurely throughout the warm summer weekends and pick blackberries right up to the end of August.

Dog walkers and groups of cyclists are not uncommon, with the latter usually appearing at weekends. On the opposite side to the towpath lock house is a small but pleasantly laid out marina. Cranfleet Lock opens out onto the Trent, which beckons us with the promise of lazy days on the river; from thereon it remains navigable, with fine views of the woodlands and foreground parklands of the Thrumpton estate to be had.

Christmas Day 2006 on the Cranfleet.

Blackberrying along the Cranfleet.

The original clubhouse of the Nottingham Sailing Club stands next to the lock-keeper's house. From here Jasper, the lean tabby cat, pads out to inspect the fence side shrubberies or seek shade on sunny mornings. He is often to be found beneath one of the recreational seats. Jasper, at the time of writing, is thirteen years old. He is a refugee from a houseboat that I believe was eventually abandoned and he arrived at the lock house during a particularly severe summer night storm. He has lived with the lock-keeper ever since.

There is a boat user's car park on the other side of the preventative hurdle. From this point a lane takes the walker and motorist between the fields and gravel extraction lakes to the superstores of Tesco and Asda in Long Eaton. The towpath itself continues, with the river on the right and masses of scrubland screening gravel extraction lakes to the left. Small birds like the summer visiting warbler species attract the birdwatchers to this spot. An early morning ramble is made even more interesting if, like me, you can differentiate between bird songs. Occasionally horses and ponies can be found grazing and paddocked beside the towpath and eventually, on rounding a long bend, a group of chalets flank the path.

Beyond the River Erewash the Trent enters the district beneath a stone and concrete bridge while a path, well trodden today, takes the rambler up to the environmental interpretative centre managed by the Nottinghamshire Wildlife Trust. Continuing along the ever-circuitous banks of the Trent, one eventually reaches Barton Island. In the 1950s the owner, whose name I never picked up, used a wooden bungalow here as a holiday home. The upstream section was occupied, perhaps on a leasehold basis, by the local Sea Scout Group.

For the naturalist there is much to see around the gravel extraction lakes of the Attenborough Nature Reserve over to the left. Footpaths wind beside the hedgerows, and by bearing left the rambler can return to the Trent path and Cranfleet Lock which both lie ahead. The towpath continues for two miles to Beeston.

On looking at the sandy banks of the Trent I am reminded of the sand martins – members of the swallow family, which nest in the holes there – and also the kingfishers. In the late 1980s eleven pairs of kingfishers nested along this stretch from Barton Island to Beeston Weir. Considering that the sandy banks are cut through by this river for a considerable length of its journey, one wonders how many pairs nest along its 170 or so miles?

Beyond the chalets, backed by water meadows at Barton-in-Fabis on the opposite side, Brands Hill rises some 285ft above the flood plain. At this point the wood blends into the Clifton and Rough woods. On the summit of Brands Hill archaeologists located a sizeable enclosure dating from the Iron Age but sadly little remains of its previous grandeur.

Next Beeston Marina comes into view; many more boats are to be found here than there were in the 1960s. Beyond the tract of willow woods a mobile home site fringes the towpath. There are chalets to the left and boats, elongated pontoons and slipways to the right.

A café, riverside bar and marina can also be found here, positioned beside a dry dock ramp and sizeable chandlers store. In the early nineteenth century rowing boats, pleasure steamers and a ferry operated from these banks. At Beeston Lock the river plunges through a weir; adjacent to the weir is a hydroelectric generator. The wooded banks of Clifton on the south side of the river were planted with deciduous trees like the oak, beech and lime between 1740 and 1742. This area, which saw the trees through to their full maturity some hundred or so years later, came to be known as Lovers Walk, especially by the Sunday-strolling Victorians and Edwardians.

Although half-screened by housing estates since the 1940s, Clifton Village is still green. Queen Anne almshouses, a dovecote and the now-derelict hall were built in late medieval times. The Clifton Campus buildings of Nottingham Trent University are discernible beyond the trees.

Opposite: A tract of the Attenborough Nature Reserve.

Left: Jasper at thirteen years of age.

Below: Where the River Erewash meets the Trent.

The lock house – there may once have been two – appears to be in good repair, and if there is no one in residence at the present time it would, as one boater observed, make a good interpretative centre. There is a British Waterways interpretative plaque beside the lock which is useful to all visitors.

Beeston Lock and the stretch of waterway leading from it has been well covered in the Tempus publication *Nottingham Canal: A History and Guide* (Bernard Chell, 2006). This, with the aforementioned publication in mind, is the point at which the Trent Lock towpath explorer should be turning back.

While sitting with a winter morning coffee in the café back along the marina path I have watched a dog fox quartering the reeded bays of the opposite bank. I have seen the cormorants both submerged and in flight and, as always, the gliding and wheeling activities of the gulls, all of which I find both intriguing and relaxing. Leaving the café and returning along the river path to Trent Lock there is, if the walker or explorer has the time, a signposted path pointing towards Beeston. This is a very old, well-used route, and was probably used as a lane between the fields before gravel extraction operations began in the late 1930s and early '40s.

The fields and land tract were, a Beeston neighbour told me, called 'The Robin Hoods' by the local folk. Here they gathered blackberry and raspberry harvests and the boys made dens whilst acting out the Tom Mix films they had seen at the local cinemas. The lane divides the gravel extraction lakes and continues across the breadth of the site to a railway crossing. It is here that the explorer or rambler should turn left, follow the path of the Attenborough Nature Reserve

The Weir Cottage Lockhouse, Beeston Lock.

Boats in Beeston Lock leaving the Trent for the Nottingham Canal.

through the willow woods and over the bridge with the wide tract of water known as The Works Pond on the right. The railway is on the far side of The Works Pond.

The narrow track winds between the thickets and waterside channel to a stile, beyond which are the splendid east-facing cottages of the Old Attenborough village. For the rambler to remain properly oriented the cricket ground needs to be on the left. Where the cricket ground ends this exploration bears left at a gate and over a bridge arm of water.

An immediate right turn needs to be made at this point which will leave a wide expanse of gravel extraction water on the left, and the reeded arm of water, a pony grazed field and church with an imposing spire to the right. The path should be followed round to the attractive little backwater on the right that often carries a perfect reflection of the church. The wide expanse of water is just one part of the 600-acre Attenborough Nature Reserve site which was officially opened in 1966. In 1982 it was declared a Site of Special Scientific Interest.

Since the first birdwatchers assembled at the Beeston end of the Reserve in the 1940s over 250 bird species have been recorded here. Amongst others dabbling, seagoing, diving duck, raptors, waders, swan and wild geese species, small migratory birds and passerines have taken full advantage of these bounteous habitats, just as those no doubt delighted members of The Nottinghamshire Wildlife Trust always intended.

On a historical note, the field alongside the church – on which the ponies graze – is known as Standard Field where, local historians insist, Parliamentarian Colonel Ireton raised his Standard during the Civil War. Over the years young equestrians saddling or feeding their ponies here claim to have seen in the dusk a 'Cavalier-type' figure strolling the gentle slope. Open-minded people have explored the possibility of the figure being the apparition of Colonel Ireton,

A coot and Canada goose pair. Nottinghamshire is overpopulated by Canada geese.

Dabbling duck species such as the mallard are also commonplace.

although he was a Parliamentarian (or Roundhead). The term 'Cavalier type' is a direct reference to the Civil War.

Where the church and backwater meet the lane this ramble or exploration bears left; by turning right one can see the church of St Mary Magdalene and the splendid old house, still occupied, where the Ireton family lived. Not surprisingly, Colon Ireton invited Cromwell here and eventually married his daughter. The christening records of Cromwell's grandaughter are displayed inside the church, which was used by Cromwell and the mounted section of his army to stable their horses. Here one needs to take a nearby path, keeping the church and backwater to the left, and continue between the gravel extraction lakes to the car park, where one should again bear left.

To the right is the newly opened interpretative and education centre, a true milestone in the social history of the Nottinghamshire Wildlife Trust. Here local wildlife species can be observed on video, with a meal and a splendid cup of coffee if required. From there the bridge needs to be negotiated and then comes the lane and the thickets, then the pony paddocks, the newly established reed beds and the lagoons before you reach the path of the River Trent.

A right turn then takes the rambler over the bridge, again where the River Erewash merges with the Trent. The route can then be retraced, with this wide river to the left and Cranfleet and Trent Locks beckoning ahead.

CHAPTER NINE
UPSTREAM OF TRENT LOCK

In recent years the downstream path from Trent Lock has been opened as part of an agreement between various authorities. I understand that British Waterways played a significant part.

The tubular gate barring the path since the 1950s has a stile and narrow walkway attached. In contrast, the gate previously bore the rather stern deterrent 'NO ENTRY'. I cannot recall having seen anyone walking the river path beyond this point. The gate may have been installed to prevent grazing cattle from straying, but in the words of one local man, 'It did its job in keeping people out.' Today the message seems to be 'walk and enjoy the river paths where possible by all means', and the feeling is that everyone equipped with a sense of exploration and love of the fresh air inwardly appreciates the freedom that is offered.

The walk between the banks of the Trent and the golf course is open to the winds and personally I find it quite delightful. It can also be taken by people of most age groups, since its destination point seems to be Sawley Lock, which is but a short distance away.

From the path the fountain centred lake and willows close to the clubhouse looks splendid. The lake, or pool as some prefer to call it, is a landscaped continuation of the long reedy watershed. The lake may have been formed by water left over and naturally channelled by past floodings, particularly those of 1947.

Narrow channels, with small neat bridges, have been cut away to join natural dykes. These were destined to eventually take any surplus water across to the river path and into the Trent. Birds like lapwing, snipe, redshank and mallard will feed both on and in such habitats. At the time of writing, and for the past two years, in fact, this has become the hunting territory of a female kestrel which quarters the ground on both sides of the river. When not quartering or hovering she can often be seen perched on top of one of the telegraph poles.

A long railway bridge and embankment almost screen the outbuildings of Sawley Lock; this runs level with the river on the opposite side. At the bridge arches a farm gate blocks the path. On my last sojourn in November 2006, although I cannot recall the wording, a notice requested that members of the public not enter the field beyond. Yet for all that, there were still people exercising their dogs in the field! Nevertheless, the notice gave me the impression that we were expected to cross the railed footbridge spanning the Trent; this lies close to where the railway bridge spans the river. This line is apparently used to carry coal to the power stations and oil to Castle Donington.

Sawley Lock is fine and well tended. There is a lock-keeper on hand if required while the public are requested not to cross the lock but rather to remain on the footpath side. The lock-keeper's cottage bears a plaque outlining the flood level mark of the year 2002. This, incidentally, is considered to be the busiest lock in the county.

A general scene at Sawley Lock.

Passing through Sawley Lock.

Sawley with towpath looking towards Trent Lock.

With a university group I parked at nearby Sawley Marina during those floodings, unaware of just how far the flood water had reached. We walked for a yard or two beyond the M1 bridge and found the area flooded throughout. The gravel extraction and angling lakes to the left could barely be told apart from the river. Only the occasional tops of a hedgerow could be seen with the rest underwater. These floods were similar to those which would have been experienced in the past, but this time homes were built further away from the affected areas. The relatively broad towpath continues down to the busy main road bridge and to the left, when traffic permits, Sawley Marina occupies an aquatic area which, in my 1950s youth held but one small gravel extraction lake. The road is busy and dangerous here and, by way of a disclaimer, I emphasise that it should be crossed with extreme care.

The bridge was constructed of iron and stone and it spans the two river forks, including the oxbow shallows below Sawley Weir. It replaces a combined bridge and causeway that, in the fifteenth century, was built to replace a ferry. The bridge is known as Harrington Bridge or – more colloquially – Harrington Arches, in recognition of local landowner the Earl of Harrington. The Harrington Arms stands on the far side of the bridge beside, but still above, the Sawley Weir field. Across the road the towpath passes beside an industrial unit which has been surrounded in recent years by a natural moat. Then, across from the tumultuous roar of the M1 bridge, built on a reinforced structure of concrete, the spire of Sawley church can be seen beyond the weir and fields to the right.

There are water meadows beyond and to the right, and privately run gravel extraction angling lakes to the left. These look particularly splendid in the sunset when one is journeying down the M1, soon to leave by the Nottingham South junction.

In the 1960s sixty or seventy Friesian cows grazed the land, which has since been reclaimed by water. At a particularly acute bend on the Trent, the river is joined by the Trent & Mersey Canal after the final lock. Here the unnavigable Derbyshire Derwent also winds in from the right.

A flood level marker on the lock-keeper's cottage.

Here, until the floodings of 2002, the aptly named Long Horse Bridge conveyed the horse and towpath walker across the Trent to the towpath of the Trent & Mersey Canal. This bridge, made of concrete and erected in 1932, replaced the earlier wooden trestle bridge which had been designed and overseen by the ultimate waterways engineer, James Brindley. Pronounced unsafe by several experts following the 2002 floodings, the bridge was dismantled a year later.

In February 2007, when I spoke with a British Waterways contact while enquiring as to whether or not an alternative bridge had been erected, I was advised that although one was planned there was not a bridge on the site of the two previous bridges. The alternative for anyone wanting to walk to Shardlow, I was told, would be to stay on the south bank of the Trent and follow it to Shardlow Mooring, where the path terminated near the Cavendish Bridge on London Road.

Like most towpath enthusiasts in this area I have my seasonal memories of this smaller 'Watersmeet', where the Trent & Mersey Canal and the Derwent join the Trent. The first that comes to mind takes me back to the March morning when the fields to the left of the Trent & Mersey footpath were swamped by floodwater. Defining this field tract from a lake were the hawthorn hedgerows striking defensively across the flood plain. I was the interested observer of a swan pair using the thickets as screens in their bid to shake off a dominant pair which pursued them, wings arched over their backs, determined to see off the intruders.

The second occurred on a September morning when two narrowboats were released from the Derwentmouth Lock, each with a man guiding them between the reedy banks while their waterproof clad wives or partners walked towards me. Each had a deep basket over one arm as they plucked the seasonal harvest of mushrooms, blackberries and wild raspberries from the towpath and hedgerows. They were the only group of boaters I saw that morning and they greeted me warmly while exuding that buoyancy of spirit that is so characteristic of those who love the great outdoors; our waterways in particular.

CHAPTER TEN

TRENT LOCK IN THE TWENTY-FIRST CENTURY

Having two pubs beside the canal, with the river in close proximity and a ferry to provide transport, Trent Lock was as popular a resort in the past as it is today. Quite a number of postcards and archive photographs support this view. The scenes depicting people beside the lock and boats are extremely crowded, to say the least. One should remember that few – if any – of these people arrived by car.

Church and social club outings by charabanc were often organised in those halcyon days of garden fêtes and skittling for a pig. The occasional landau or single-decker bus may also have brought people in, but I doubt whether they came from long distances. Most visitors would have been local people walking Lock Lane from Wilne and Sawley. Others would have been strollers who dropped in on their way to Long Eaton and Sandiacre, perhaps Toton.

People walked to places in the early 1900s, just as my parents walked. Some carried picnic hampers. Angling was as popular then as it is today, but more of its practitioners used the term 'fishing'. Rowing boats – whereby couples and families paid sixpence or a shilling to have a boat out on the river – were very popular, and you were more likely to see a dozen rowing boats on the river than two or three, particularly on Bank Holiday weekends. Pleasure boats which were equipped to carry thirty or forty people at a time may have taken visitors and local folk up the Cranfleet or downstream to Sawley Lock. One can imagine the boatman with the loud hailer standing on the slipway calling out to the crowds as those passengers already seated in the boat waited for it to fill up. Of course this meant waiting until the boatman had decided that he had enough people on board to warrant a journey. There would have been soft drink sellers and ice-cream men, while a galloping horses roundabout would perhaps have been sited on the lawns of The Navigation.

Those early sepia photographs emphasise the styles of dress of the straw boaters, wide brimmed hats worn by women and the picnic baskets they carried. Most, if not all, of the men wore suits. The women wore the almost obligatory tunic jacket with a long pleated skirt. The men sported jackets and trousers with matching waistcoats. Their headgear was usually a trilby or bowler. They took snuff and carried a gold watch and chain in the waistcoat pocket.

The majority of the suits worn by these men, heavily attired even on hot days, would have been sombre in colour, most likely brown, charcoal grey or black. The more youthful men and women may have settled for light grey or fawn. Anyone wearing a boater and striped jacket was looked upon as a show-off, akin to an off-duty music hall star, while children were often made to wear sun hats.

When professional boatmen and lock-keepers met with day trippers, the majority of those who did not spend their lives on the waterways lined up to stand, stare and wave when they saw

Above: Trent Lock in the twenty-first century.

Left: Trent Navigation sign.

a narrowboat passing through a lock. Factory hands and lace or textile mill workers from Long Eaton or Sandiacre flocked to the lock, the pubs and the river, and deservedly so. These were hardworking people, living in difficult times, and they had earned their leisure periods.

The canal towpath on those summer weekend evenings would have been busy with people, families and couples. I imagine them making their way home with picnic hampers empty and their money spent. People were less inclined to visit such places in wartime, although hot weekend days would surely have tempted them out, even if only for short spells.

While researching Trent Lock in the early twentieth century I came across an entry stating that the venue had attracted 1,000 people in 1944. By modern standards this is not an enormous figure, but considering the fact that people mostly walked or rode bicycles it stands as a testament to the popularity of Trent Lock. It also speaks of people's need to be close to water and to breath air untainted by the mills and factories of nearby Long Eaton.

On some of the sepia photographs I viewed there were at least sixty people crowded around the lock or rowing boat slipway. From these photographs I inferred that people may well have visited Trent Lock in their thousands on pre-war weekends. The Navigation and The Steamboat pubs were probably as busy then as they are today. They were supplied by deliveries from the brewery; these were made by horses and dreys, and they came in all weathers and travelled along the narrow and winding Lock Lane to one or the other of these hostelries.

Extroverts flourished at this time and in this situation, whether they were behind the hostelry bars or on the narrowboats. Widely regarded as 'characters', these people were colourful with vivid tales to tell and they enjoyed exchanging their stories with like-minded people. I imagine that the pubs, bars and lounges had the kind of cigarette and tobacco-filled, smoky atmosphere that encourages vibrant conversation. The mind's eye conjures up an image of a wide variety of ales and a low but continual hum of voices as men greeted their fellows, exchanged experiences and viewpoints, cajoled, connived and argued. Most waterside pubs and the occasional lock-keeper also made a tidy little business out of catering for the anglers, or fishermen as they would have been called at the time. The pubs provided both the lunchtime snacks and the breakfasts for the fishermen. Hearty meals of eggs, bacon, tomatoes, beans and fried bread with mugs of tea to follow were provided for the hungry hordes. An elderly Long Eaton woman, who had served at The Steamboat (probably then known as The Fisherman's Rest), once told me that:

> It was a sideline income but one that paid off handsomely on those weekend summer mornings in the fishing season.

Around the pubs you could also find horse boys and porters. Their duties included ensuring that the paths by the locks, stableyards and those fronting the pubs were cleared of horse manure. Until the Second World War horse manure was not regarded as waste – this was an attitude that prevailed throughout the country. Instead it was swept into buckets, sometimes to be sold to people who had gardens or allotments and put horse manure onto their plant or vegetable plots. One can also imagine there being free-range poultry around the lock-keeper's cottage and pub yard as well as a goat or two for milking.

In the late 1930s, with the canal temporarily unused, people still visited the pubs and walked the towpaths. However, this was usually only at the weekends. The comparative few who lived near the lock often became pub regulars and thus the bond between landlord and customer held, but the ties were looser than they had been in the past. By the end of the 1940s the brewery orders were delivered by lorry while come the end of the 1950s the first motoring families were looking for somewhere to park their cars; likewise with the anglers.

The Lockhouse Tearooms.

I have stated in a previous chapter that there were few people to be seen around on weekdays. Obviously the majority were working. However, come the mid-1960s cars were parking on the land which had been designated as a car park at the end of Lock Lane as well as behind the private residence.

Strollers used to walk along the path directly in front of the windows of this residence. As a casual observer I thought this audacious. In a bold move I tried it myself several times and was always careful to keep my eyes on the pond when I passed. As I had come to expect of this stretch of riverbank there was no one around. There came a morning when I swung around the front corner of the house intending to walk the path and met with a gaunt, but nevertheless awesome, Great Dane. As I turned away I knew that the owner of the property, without so much as raising a finger, was making a point. In more recent years, the property has had electrically controlled gates installed. In the disturbing times in which we are living that is perhaps understandable.

Trent Lock slowly regained its popularity and the number of pleasure boaters increased. This was in part due to people retiring early and also to the numbers of people working shifts. Members of the public walk the towpaths with the blessing of the ever-watchful British Waterways departments and local Environment Agencies. The sense of freedom and leisure which one feels in Trent Lock helps to place it high on the local list of interesting and pleasurable places to visit. Surely more people now live on houseboats, or pass through as they explore our network of waterways? Most of the residents agree upon this point.

I am told of people living in the area who are in their eighties and remember the bombings during the war. There are also retired lengthmen, while many people are currently employed as waterways maintenance men. But the longest established family must surely be the Mills, the family who run the dockyard. A sign by Lock Lane accommodation bridge advertises the fact that they have been at Trent Lock since 1890. Perhaps their ancestors were working here before that time. A member of the Erewash Canal Preservation and Development Society pointed out that the Mills family bought the current, long-established site from the Erewash Canal Company. Clearly tradition has not been lost here because the Mills have, I am assured, run the dockyard, boat building and maintenance business since that time. It is now run by Steve Mills.

The public car park as we know it today was laid out complete with new toilet blocks around 1972–73, and although the lane remains narrow, it helps in curbing the would-be speed enthusiasts. It is maintained by the Erewash Borough Council. The Trent Lock Golf Centre has had a surprisingly positive effect on the landscape and leisure scene. This obviously brings files of steady traffic to Lock Lane, but in the twenty-first century this is only to be expected.

Built in 1992, the clubhouse is splendid and spacious. Adjacent to the reception area is the Pro Shop, which extends to 6,000 square feet. There are various bars, along with a restaurant, wedding and civic ceremony areas, with dancing and a Master of Ceremonies if required, not to mention conference facilities. Parties and special occasions can be catered for. There is also a Nicklaus Suite which comfortably holds 200 or more people.

Members of the public, non-golfers as they are described in the glossy brochure, are also welcome. The 'Riverside' eighteen-hole course is designed for golfers in general, while the nine-hole course is, according to a member of staff, a pay-and-play course particularly suited to beginners. It is in golfing parlance a par thirty-six course extending for 2,911 yards.

Lock Lane was once a black screened road, perhaps lit in winter along the canal bank by moored boats and chalets. Today the lane has the same length, width and shape, but is lit consistently by the elongated trail of headlights as drinkers, dancers and diners carefully walk in file around the bends to and from the golf club and the pubs beyond. The Steamboat in particular holds special event type evenings which, I am assured, are well attended. It is also a diner's venue, with a range of ales and beers on offer; on particularly cold nights a blazing fire can be found in the hearth. Mark and Terry Ashby, the owners and proprietors of the Lock House Tearooms, fulfilled an ambition when the lock-keeper's house and home for many generations became empty.

The local councillors had previously agreed to the house (and former toll payments office) becoming tearooms with artwork, ceramic designs and artefacts of waterways' life clearly displayed. Many eyes rest, I have noticed, on the Buckby cans that bring so much colour. They also contribute to a traditional atmosphere, and a sense that the rituals of the narrowboat scene are being maintained.

Tradition is also a primary consideration in the tearoom's interior, where antiques and collectables are put on sale and can be seen on request. Over the past 200 or so years hand-painted canalware featuring roses and castles – recognised as English folk art – has been handed down from family to family, boatyard to boatyard, and is also well to the fore.

The explanatory leaflet *Lock House Tearooms: And canal historic centre*, portrays each member of the Ashby family as an inter-complementary artist: Mark is an award-winning chap who creates old-fashioned culinary delights, while his wife Terry is, when time and chance permit, a graphic designer and traditional folk painter.

In the main tearooms there are mugs hanging from hooks and displays of bygone cigarette and tobacco brands. There are plates, hats, antlers, canal memorabilia and corners devoted to the framed pictures and photographs of the waterways scene, as well as an interesting display featuring 'Waterways at War'.

On the shelves are displayed types of old lamps, including the Kelly lamp, vases, bottles, and so on. and not forgetting in one corner a sewing machine, flat iron and gramophone. Beside

Opposite above:
The Lockhouse
Tearoom's interior.

Opposite below:
'The Olde Worlde' on
display.

Right: A welcoming
atmosphere.

the private family staircase, which faces the front door, stand waxwork models depicting a 'canal age' family in traditional dress.

From newspaper cuttings, I learned that the Lock House Tearooms were officially opened by the Mayor and Mayoress of Erewash on 29 July 1996. The civic couple arrived after alighting from a car at the Tamworth Road canal bridge and after the formal introductions travelled in the 45ft narrowboat *Ashby Castle* for the short but pleasant trip to Trent Lock where after the official opening they were presented with a traditional Buckby can.

The Lock House Tearooms rightfully boast of providing '50 different teas or fresh ground coffee', a range of cakes and salads, and 'the biggest Knickerbocker Glory this side of the Trent!' Much though I look forward to my occasional cup of coffee there, I quietly revel in the atmosphere of history and tradition that is so colourfully portrayed on either side.

Left: A Buckby Can.

Below: From far distant times…

A railway notice from 1901.

ON THE TOWPATHS

Throughout these times of early retirement lone walkers, groups and couples make their way along the towpaths extending from Beeston Lock or the Attenborough Reserve car park to Trent Lock and the Lock House Tearooms. Fewer, perhaps, stroll down from the Cranfleet car park.

In the Bank Holidays the numbers are swollen by the families, sometimes three generations, eager to visit that seemingly essential 'somewhere different'. Around Trent Lock boaters converse with ramblers, canal maintenance men with artists and anglers, bar-keeping staff with photographers, birdwatchers and connoisseurs of home brewed ale. Sages, grey haired and bearded, reminisce about visits to Trent Lock when they were young and members of varied waterway preservation societies discuss moorings, lock chambers and the adventures of late colleagues as portrayed by the local waterway journals.

Preservation is again the keyword in the times of which I am writing and, of course, waterways maintenance. Nonetheless, in the bars and tearooms and beside the slipways, locks and moorings, the atmosphere is convivial, to say the least, as people with differing talents and interests meet and discuss the prospects of Trent Lock in the twenty-first century.

CHAPTER ELEVEN

TRENT & MERSEY CANAL

I knew nothing of the inland port of Shardlow until the mid-1960s. Then one midsummer afternoon I followed the towpath from the Harrington Arms bridge, left the Trent as I crossed The Longhorse Bridge and rounded the bends of the Trent & Mersey Canal. Beyond the A6 bridge was a lock and derelict wharf, alongside which stood the building that we know today as the Clock Warehouse.

The building was fascinating in its structure but the overriding impression was that it was drab and derelict. Swallows and house martins 'hawked' for flies and undoubtedly had nests in and about the building, while a pair of swans had a nest in the screening reeds. Otherwise there was not a sign of life. I was literally the only man on the towpath. I briefly wondered about the future of this and other such abandoned wharves, little realising that some forty years later there would be afternoons when I would be sitting outside that same building by the willows, taking sips from a pint of Marstons bitter.

On that first visit I tried to make sense of the smaller, surrounding buildings. Boat repair workshops? Stabling for those long-forgotten towpath horses? Blacksmiths? Farriers? Paint sheds? It was almost impossible to imagine there having been people here. People would have been working by daylight and Kelly lamp. The wealthy, the healthy, the sick and the poor. It was difficult to think of this place as having nurtured a thriving community; the absence of both community and industry gave the place a silent, almost ethereal atmosphere from which one could not escape the sense of time passing.

Later in the 1960s my wife and I would drive out from Beeston to Shardlow on what were regularly stifling Sunday evenings, and visit the bars of The Malt Shovel. There were people; there were cars; and there were what we thought of as pleasure boats journeying the Trent & Mersey Canal. Quite obviously other people had 'discovered' Shardlow. Something was afoot.

INFLUENCE OF THE TRENT & MERSEY CANAL

Although on that first visit I realised that Shardlow was different, it was not until I began scanning the Derbyshire guides and boating magazines that I realised it was amongst the earliest of the inland waterway ports. By the 1970s it was regarded as a waterways showcase, and boaters were urged to moor where possible and look around Shardlow, either on their exit from the Trent & Mersey Canal or during their explorations.

Above: Shardlow Basin with the Clock Warehouse.

Left: Shardlow Lock on the Trent & Mersey Canal.

This waterway of ninety-two or so miles extended from Derwent Mouth to Preston Brook and has been described as 'the dream child' of James Brindley. He had an idea for a waterway network that he called 'The Grand Cross'; he envisaged this linking the Thames with the Severn, the Mersey and the Humber. Josiah Wedgwood, who established pottery works in Staffordshire, had a similar idea.

In 1766 the first promotional Act of Parliament was passed and over the next sixty years a further nine acts followed. At first the waterway was called the Grand Trunk Canal. Unfortunately, James Brindley died five years before its completion. Along a stretch of it could be found the Harecastle Tunnel, which was perhaps unique in terms of canal-building in this period. It extended for 2,897 yards and took eleven years to dig out. The entire stretch of the Trent & Mersey Canal was opened in 1777 and commercially this waterway proved highly successful..

Staffordshire pottery was one main and continual cargo conveyed along the route, the other was coal because Staffordshire had its coalfields and Cheshire its salt mines. Beer was also conveyed from the breweries at Burton-on-Trent. In 1784 a share bought for £200 was by 1824 valued at £2,400. Only a matter of years later shareholders revelled in pay-out dividends of around 75 per cent.

In present times the canal is still busy with cruisers. Along the route are waterside pubs and restaurants intersected by marinas and boatyards.

Many of the place names listed in the distant tables of waterway publications are also interesting, to say the least.

THE CLOCK WAREHOUSE

The Clock Warehouse stands beside Shardlow Lock and its pub surroundings undoubtedly have visiting boaters checking around for moorings. Several types of cargo craft were to be seen there throughout the thriving days of the canal age, including the Yorkshire or Humber type sailing keel usually worked by the Trent Navigation Company. The keel was actually a barge, double-ended and sporting but with one mast.

The beam of 14ft 6in prevented the vessel from journeying the canal, although the length was 58ft. A keel could carry up to 90 cargo tons and was therefore invaluable to the company concerned. However, transhipment was necessary. Barges like the keel were unloaded and the narrowboats loaded. A warehouse of any description had to be used because there was much sorting and resorting to be done, often before the reloading could take place. Here, then was another form of employment and unless one had the enviable task of clerk and day bookkeeper, it was continual but back-breaking work.

Most of the loaders and unloaders, the transhipment labourers lived locally. Probably in Shardlow itself. There were loaders and unloaders, perhaps interchanging duties; porters and general warehousemen, intermingling with boatmen; blacksmiths, ropemakers, teamsters and horse boys, along with supervisors from the firms – potteries, breweries, maltsters and ironworks – checking on the required consignments.

Shardlow village in 1789 had a population of around 300. By 1840–45 there was a work-orientated increase of close on 1,400. Businesses thrived, the carrier and merchant companies made money. The Cavendish Bridge Boat Company was not one of them. It was deemed a failure, in 1781 being put on the market due to bankruptcy despite holding a fleet of twenty boats.

The Clock Warehouse was known in those days as 'B' Warehouse and was built in 1780. The warehouse was designed with an inlet and loading, each giving the building an atmosphere of distinction.

What are now bar and restaurant rooms were once storerooms, in those days on ground level and above. As they were fashioned, cranes, jibs and hoists would have been placed at strategic places appertaining to the loading and unloading positions. Yet for all its architectural forethought and design, the name of the architect or architects remains a mystery to this day.

Doubtless there will be some waterway historian making comparisons as she or he explores warehouses as they travel the many and varied routes. It is an interesting project, perhaps almost as taxing on one's spare time as it was for those twenty or so inland historians, each of whom claim to have found the 'true identity' of Robin Hood. Except that the Clock Warehouse at Shardlow is really only known to people travelling the waterways, therefore if the name of a suspected architect is ever uncovered it will in all probability be the definitive one.

There were alterations over the years, especially since ale, malt, oats, barley and surprisingly a wide variety of cheeses were transhipped and stored hereabout, though whether foodstuffs were actually stored in the Clock Warehouse no one can say. They probably were. These items did, after all, need to be stored somewhere.

Coal, limestone, gypsum, lead, iron and pottery came on the boats through and to Shardlow, all of which needed to be stored; and pottery was a prime Staffordshire cargo travelling the Trent & Mersey for many years.

For long recognised as an inland port, Shardlow was the storage depot of other warehouses, among which was the Iron Warehouse. The name alone interests the historians of present times.

In the nearby pubs, probably better known as 'inns' in the time of which I am writing, were quarters of the flyboat teams just as the Ashbys at the Lock House Tearooms, Trent Lock, have interpreted in the basement of that intriguing property.

Flyboat teams and their horses stayed overnight at those inns or hostelries with such accommodation and changed crews there, while travelling day and night with particular consignments that were considered top priority and therefore agreed upon.

On the north bank of the Trent & Mersey was a wharf from which the packet boat service run by the Sutton family operated and for a time, on Sundays, took Shardlow's religious residents to the All Saints Church at Aston-on-Trent. There were by contrast, and as would be expected, several public houses, the busiest perhaps having been The Canal Tavern.

This was built beside Shardlow Lock and the lock-keepers from the cottages or opposite had only to cross those all too familiar lock gates to reach the bar of their choosing.

At the Interpretative Centre I learned that this pub closed in 1963 and is now a private residence with windows looking out onto the gleaming meanders of the Trent. No one was allowed to 'go without' here, I was told. All forms of butchered meat could be bought and bread freshly baked on the premises.

Crossing Shardlow Bridge for a look at the loading arch of the Clock Warehouse one passes The Old Salt Warehouse with plaques appertaining to its purpose. The bridge is part of the old turnpike road connecting London to the stern of a replica wide boat, the *Derbyshire Lass* and is on display. Inside the pub is a small but compact gallery where the framed prints of different types of boats are worth looking at. Friends, have pointed out when by the loading arch, how small were the bricks that were used for building the Clock Warehouse.

Usually I re-cross the canal bridge here with Shardlow Lock and the warehouse to my right. The Heritage Centre is close to the roadside wall, fronting a curve of the wharf. It is, I should add, run by a group of really dedicated and knowledgeable volunteers and open only at the weekends and during Bank Holiday. Here maps and pamphlets on canal history are displayed and photographs can be perused.

Shardlow Basin and Wharf.

Once a salt warehouse, now the Interpretative Centre.

Stern of a replica wide boat.

Just before turning down Canalside and going under the bridge with my back to the Clock Tower Warehouse, I usually pause to look at the fading notice on the brickwork stating that E. Stevens dealt in flour, fertilisers and corn from those premises. There are warehouses once owned by this family on both sides of the road. On a recent visit it was also good to see a class of Derbyshire schoolchildren exploring the wharves and buildings and making notes and comparisons as part of a project.

CHAPTER TWELVE

SHARDLOW'S PUBS AND VILLAGE

The financial doomsday of the Trent & Mersey Canal occurred when the company realised that they could not compete with the North Staffordshire Railway and their definitive action of rooting their tracks, as near as possible, along the course of the canal.

By 1846 the Trent & Mersey Company had sold out to the North Staffordshire Railway. The railway company still used the canal while being acutely aware of the consistent fall off in trade and thereby daily use. By 1895 the Trent & Mersey Canal was termed a low-level income operation. In 1923 when Britain's railways were regionally divided into four companies, the waterway was managed by the London Midland and Scottish Railway. This company made known their beliefs that all canal trading should come to an end. However, salt was still transported along the Trent & Mersey and also gravel. In 1948 an act relating to railway nationalisation was to some extent favoured by a subsidiary of the British Transport Commission. The subsidiary was called the Docks and Inland Waterways Department in respect of maintaining the navigational routes of Great Britain.

By 1960, however, the last consignment of salt had been delivered to the Shardlow warehouses and in 1962 the final consignment of gravel was steered into a relatively quiet wharf. Then, as is the story with most, if not all, of our waterways, the Trent & Mersey, with Shardlow splendidly and rightfully included, was rescued through the renewed interest in pleasure boating.

SOME PROMINENT SHARDLOW FAMILIES

In 1978 Shardlow became a conservation area. There was much by way of warehouses with bay and semi-circular windows, the canal pubs and wharfs, and in the village some quite splendid properties of Georgian design.

As one walks along the towpath with one's back to the A6, the walled rear garden of The Lady in Grey, a hotel, still retains its area of seclusion even though its notice invites the public to come in and sample its hospitalities. In the days of the prospering merchants and gentry this was the home of the Soresby family, of the boat-owning partnership Soresby and Flack.

There is nearby a private house that was once the ropemaking factory of a family called the Henshalls. And from Broughton House, canal transporter James Sutton moved with his family to the more prestigious residency of Shardlow Hall.

Shardlow Bridge and the old salt warehouse.

In the late seventeenth century the Fossbrooke family accepted the lease of the Wilden Ferry as offered by Thomas Coke who resided at Melbourne Hall. In 1743 there occurred a financial disappointment when Leonard Fossbrooke lost the lease which was transferred to a group of Derby businessmen.

Not to be outdone, the Fossbrookes never lost sight of that lease and in 1758 Leonard Fossbrooke regained it even though a bridge was being built close by.

Another business opportunity was gained locally when in the early eighteenth century James Sutton bought the profitable salt works from William Moore of Wychdon Lodge and the salt works at Weston-on-Trent were by the 1820s producing an output of 250 tons each week.

STROLLING AROUND THE VILLAGE

So interesting is the towpath and histories on the short walk between the A6 bridge and the village main street bridge, that one can be forgiven for thinking only in terms of the Trent & Mersey Canal and its traffic, past and present. Shardlow boasts a village green and cricket ground like most other villages, although neither are within sight of the waterway.

Busy days still on the Trent & Mersey.

Typical twenty-first-century view on the Trent & Mersey.

Buttresses of the original Cavendish Bridge, in a private garden.

To see something of the inner village, as I think of it, one should cross the bridge and turn with the road so that the canal is to the left and the pubs to the right.

The Malt Shovel, with the malt warehouse attached, was built in 1799. In the adjacent building lived the warehouse manager. The New Inn, by contrast, was built twenty-two years earlier in 1777 which was the year the Trent & Mersey Canal was considered fully operational.

The pub and waterway road curves right at that splendidly developed homestead called The Old Dockyard with in the background the distinctive wharf that is best viewed from the canal towpath. I hasten to add that The Old Dockyard is a private residence.

There is a twitchel and a turn left. Here the buildings lived in by the workers and employees can be compared to those of the merchants.

Long Row was formerly Cowlishaws' Row, the Cowlishaws being were a family about whom I have currently found little. But here in Shardlow the rich were known to the poor and vice-versa. They met on the roads and streets. Loaders, warehousemen and porters, blacksmiths, stable boys, would be on the towpaths and pavements with the Fossbrookes or Suttons passing or pulling in by coach. There was obvious class distinction but in so small a place everyone but everyone knew everyone else's business. This interlinking of classes through wealth and employment has intrigued many social historians and in the 1980s and '90s I skim-read a few novels relating to the subject which, even yet I do not think has been fully covered.

Over to the right is the cricket ground adjacent to the village green. Did the workers play the land-and-factory-owning families? I sometimes wonder. Shardlow Antiques have a business premises over to the left where soon after another turn left takes one again onto the A6 – or London Road – with the Clock Tower Warehouse and Wharf over to the right. Usually I cross

TOLLS taken at the
BRIDGE by Virtue of an Act of Parliament
being the same that were taken at the Ferry Viz

	s d	
Coaches, Chariots, Landaus &c; with 4 Wheels each	2„6	Double Horse, Mule, or Ass, not drawing
Chaise, Chair &c; with 2 Wheels	1„0	Hogs, and Swine, Pr Score
Waggon, Wain &c; with 4 Wheels	1„6	Sheep or Lambs, Pr Score
Cart, Wain &c; with 2 Wheels	1„0	Cows or Horned=Cattle each
Horse, Mule, or Ass, not drawing	0„1	Foot=Passengers each
		Soldiers (favour'd) each

Toll charges on a plinth. This was recovered from the Trent after floods of 1947 caused the tollbridge to collapse.

the road here and continue along the A6 for a short distance. Over to the right are the meanders of the River Trent, with two or three small islets visible during lower water levels but covered for months during high water winters.

Eventually, a more elongated bend or so from Shardlow, one arrives at Cavendish Bridge. There are traffic lights at the present bridge crossing the Trent and a county boundary sign explaining the fact that Derbyshire begins there or at the better known Shardlow, and Leicestershire strikes away to the east and south towards Loughborough or Castle Donington.

Built in 1760, the Cavendish toll bridge stood for almost 200 years until the severity of the floods following hard on the winter of 1947 first loosened then wrecked a pier and the bridge, almost unbelievably, collapsed. In a lay-by a slate pediment once positioned over the long demolished tollhouse is displayed for all to see. The tollhouse, incidentally, was demolished with the remains of the bridge that could be hauled from the riverbed.

By 1956 the single-file Bailey Bridge was installed, hence the need for traffic lights. There is a small village and pub down the slope from the bridge end and with some properties still close to the river. I have not spoken with anyone here but believe there may be some interesting accounts to be gleaned, nevertheless. On either side of the A6, immediately inside the Leicestershire border, are water channelled meadows and gravel extraction lakes. Beyond them the twenty-first century has closed in and there are traffic islands, roads and bypasses taking motor transport travellers to the south, east and west.

A short way back up the A6, where the Trent curves noticeably from Derwent Mouth, is the relatively new and smart looking Shardlow Marina. There is a chalet park attached. As a non-boater I was tempted to explore this neat and informal aquatic area one summer afternoon and decided that it

Shardlow Marina. Privately owned, it was established about thirty years ago.

A reminder of the bygone canal horses.

New Year's Day, 2006. *Piscean Lady* and neighbour at Trent Lock.

New Year greetings at Trent Lock.

is a place to which I could regularly return when I am searching, not for interesting paragraphs, but for peace. There is a disclaimer notice referring mainly to wanderers like myself in respect of accident but the café and bar are open to the public and I have found the residents friendly and welcoming.

Back along the A6 and returning to the towpath striking towards Derwent Mouth I find Chapel Marina which was once a tract of grazing land.

If the canal builders were to somehow return, would they approve of the way our canals and rivers are being used today? I feel that they would wholeheartedly; so long as the boaters of present times continue their enthusiastic contributions towards the splendid legacy of our waterways then the links between a hardworking past and a leisure-seeking future will remain resolute and serve as a reminder of the brilliant engineers who designed them and those many stalwart men, unnamed and long forgotten, who dug them out.

BIBLIOGRAPHY

Ashby, Mark and Terry, *The Lock House Tearooms, Menu and Information* (1996)

Burton, Anthony, *The Canal Builders* (April 1993, M.&M. Baldwin)

The Erewash Canal (6th Edition 2000, ECC and DA)

Heath, J., *A Look at Shardlow Past* (1978, Paddock Publications)

Lindsay, Jean, *The Trent and Mersey Canal* (1979, David & Charles)

Lord, Peter, *Portrait of the River Trent* (August 1968, Robert Hale)

Ware, Michael E., *Canals and Waterways* (1995, History In Camera, Shire Publications)

Yorke, Stan, *English Canals Explained* (2003, Countryside Books)

Other titles published by Tempus

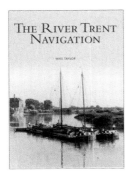

River Trent Navigation
MIKE TAYLOR

For many decades, the Trent Navigation was an essential part of Nottinghamshire's main link with London. Mike Taylor shows through over 200 illustrations how the craft and power for movement of cargoes have developed over the past century from wooden vessles using wind, tide, horses and/or human beings.

978 0 7524 1743 1

Nottingham Canal: A History and Guide
BERNARD CHELL

The Nottingham Canal, running from Trent Bridge to join with the Cromford and Erewash canals at Langley Mill, was abandoned in the 1930s but this detailed book provides a lasting record of its journey from past to present. This is the ideal companion for those interested in the history of Nottingham as well as for anyone who might be unaware how much things have changed alongside this overlooked waterway.

978 0 7524 3759 0

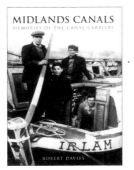

Midlands Canals: Memories of the Canal Carriers
ROBERT DAVIES

This superbly researched and illustrated book is a compilation of interviews with a handful of the folk who worked the canals during the final decades of commercial canal carrying, and captures the flavour of this lost era. The book spans the 1930s to 1960s, a time when transport of goods and materials went through great changes. It explores other topics such as the winter use of ice boats. These small but sturdy craft operated in the most hazardous conditions in order to keep the canals open.

978 0 7524 3910 5

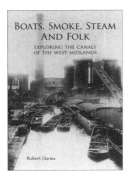

Boats, Smoke, Steam and Folk: Exploring the Canals of the West Midlands
ROBERT DAVIES

Exploring the canals of the Midlands, this book will encourage the reader to move from his armchair and into this living piece of history. It answers some of the many questions asked today about our canal network: Who did all the work; when and why were they built; what was it like to work on canals, either repairing them or moving goods about? Included are interviews and memories of those who worked on the canals.

978 0 7524 1765 3

If you are interested in purchasing other books published by Tempus, or in case you have difficulty finding any Tempus books in your local bookshop, you can also place orders directly through our website

www.tempus-publishing.com